CLASSICS *for* YOUNG READERS

Volume 8

Editor: John Holdren

Art Director: Steve Godwin

Designer: Megan Dubbs

Cover Illustrator: John Moffitt

ISBN: 1-931728-54-2

Printed by Worzalla, Stevens Point, WI, USA, June 2014, LOT 062014

TABLE OF CONTENTS

AUTOBIOGRAPHICALLY SPEAKING

STORIES IN VERSE

SHORT STORIES

To Everything There Is a Season

Making Us See

Voices and Viewpoints

THE BIBLE AS LITERATURE

POETRY OF IDEAS

TWO GREAT SPEECHES

DRAMA: AN ANCIENT TRAGEDY

AUTOBIOGRAPHICALLY SPEAKING

A CUB PILOT
by Mark Twain

You may already know Mark Twain as the author of The Adventures of Tom Sawyer. *Mark Twain was born in 1835 as Samuel Langhorne Clemens. In his autobiographical book,* Life on the Mississippi, *he wrote, "When I was a boy, there was but one permanent ambition among my comrades in our village on the west bank of the Mississippi River. That was to be a steamboatsman. Other ambitions faded out, each in its turn; but the ambition to be a steamboatsman always remained."*

*When he was little more than twenty years old, Clemens achieved his boyhood ambition—he became a riverboat pilot. A riverboat pilot steers ships in and out of port, often through dangerous waters. In order to keep the ship from running aground, it's important for the pilot to remain constantly aware of the depth of the water. In Clemens's time, the water's depth was measured by throwing in a line with a lead weight attached—which is why the men who read the line were called "leadsmen." When a leadsman measured a depth of two fathoms—a fathom is six feet—he would cry out, "Mark twain!" (*Twain *is an old-fashioned word for "two.") That cry gave Clemens the pen name by which we know him best.*

The following selection is from Mark Twain's Life on the Mississippi.

---

pilot: a person employed to steer a ship in and out of port, often through dangerous waters; a "cub pilot" is a pilot in training

There is one faculty which a pilot must incessantly cultivate until he has brought it to absolute perfection. Nothing short of perfection will do. That faculty is memory. He cannot stop with merely thinking a thing is so and so; he must *know* it; for this is one of the "exact" sciences. With what scorn a pilot was looked upon, in the old times, if he ever ventured to deal in that feeble phrase, "I think," instead of the vigorous one, "I know!"

One cannot easily realize what a tremendous thing it is to know every trivial detail of twelve hundred miles of river and know it with absolute exactness. If you will take the longest street in New York and travel up and down it, conning its features patiently until you know every house and window and lamppost and big and little sign by heart, and know them so accurately that you can instantly name the one you are abreast of when you are set down at random in that street in the middle of an inky black night, you will then have a tolerable notion of the amount and the exactness of a pilot's knowledge who carries the Mississippi River in his head. And then, if you will go on until you know every street crossing, the character, size, and position of the crossing stones, and the varying depth of mud in each of these numberless places, you

---

faculty: ability; skill
incessantly: constantly; unceasingly
cultivate: to develop; to improve by labor, care, or study
ventured: attempted; took the chance
vigorous: strong; powerful
conning: studying; examining closely
abreast: beside; alongside
tolerable: acceptable; good enough
notion: idea; concept; understanding

will have some idea of what the pilot must know in order to keep a Mississippi steamer out of trouble. Next, if you will take half of the signs in that long street, and *change their places* once a month, and still manage to know their new positions accurately on dark nights, and keep up with these repeated changes without making any mistakes, you will understand what is required of a pilot's peerless memory by the fickle Mississippi.

I think a pilot's memory is about the most wonderful thing in the world. To know the Old and New Testaments by heart and be able to recite them glibly, forward or backward, or begin at random anywhere in the book and recite both ways and never trip or make a mistake, is no extravagant mass of knowledge, and no marvelous facility, compared to a pilot's massed knowledge of the Mississippi and his marvelous facility in the handling of it. I make this comparison deliberately and believe I am not expanding the truth when I do it. Many will think my figure too strong, but pilots will not.

A pilot must have a memory, but there are two higher qualities which he must also have. He must have good and quick judgment and decision, and a cool, calm courage that no peril can shake. Give a man the merest trifle of pluck to start with, and by the time he has become a pilot, he cannot be unmanned by any danger a steamboat can get into; but one cannot quite say the same for judgment. Judgment is a matter of brains, and a man must *start* with a good stock of that article, or he will never succeed as a pilot.

---

peerless: unmatched; superior beyond comparison
fickle: likely to change without warning; unpredictable
glibly: with casual, offhand ease
facility: effortless skill; ease in performance
pluck: courage; determination
unmanned: dispirited; discouraged

The growth of courage in the pilot-house is steady all the time, but it does not reach a high and satisfactory condition until some time after the young pilot has been "standing his own watch" alone and under the staggering weight of all the responsibilities connected with the position. When the apprentice has become pretty thoroughly acquainted with the river, he goes clattering along so fearlessly with his steamboat, night or day, that he presently begins to imagine that it is *his* courage that animates him; but the first time the pilot steps out and leaves him to his own devices, he finds out it was the other man's. He discovers that the article has been left out of his own cargo altogether. The whole river is bristling with dangers in a moment; he is not prepared for them; he does not know how to meet them; all his knowledge forsakes him; and within fifteen minutes he is as white as a sheet and scared almost to death. Therefore pilots wisely train these cubs by various strategic tricks to look danger in the face a little more calmly. A favorite way of theirs is to play a friendly swindle upon the candidate.

Mr. Bixby, my chief, served me in this fashion once, and for years afterward I used to blush, even in my sleep, when I thought of it. I had become a good steersman; so good, indeed, that I had all the work to do on our watch, night and day. Mr. Bixby seldom made a suggestion to me; all he ever did was to take the wheel on particularly bad nights or in particularly bad crossings, land the boat when she needed to be landed, play gentleman of leisure nine-tenths of the watch, and collect the wages. The lower river was about bank-full, and if anybody had questioned my ability to run any crossing between Cairo

---

forsakes: abandons
swindle: fraud; trick
steersman: one who steers a ship
Cairo: a city in Illinois, where the Mississippi River is joined by the Ohio River

and New Orleans without help or instruction, I should have felt irreparably hurt. The idea of being afraid of any crossing in the lot, in the *daytime*, was a thing too preposterous for contemplation. Well, one matchless summer's day I was bowling down the bend above Island 66, brimful of self-conceit and carrying my nose as high as a giraffe's, when Mr. Bixby said,

"I am going below awhile. I suppose you know the next crossing?"

This was almost an affront. It was about the plainest and simplest crossing in the whole river. One couldn't come to any harm, whether he ran it right or not; and as for depth, there never had been any bottom there. I knew all this, perfectly well.

"Know how to *run* it? Why, I can run it with my eyes shut."

"How much water is there in it?"

"Well, that is an odd question. I couldn't get bottom there with a church steeple."

"You think so, do you?"

The very tone of the question shook my confidence. That was what Mr. Bixby was expecting. He left, without saying anything more. I began to imagine all sorts of things. Mr. Bixby, unknown to me, of course, sent somebody down to the forecastle with some mysterious instructions to the leadsmen, another messenger was sent to whisper among the officers, and then Mr. Bixby went into hiding behind a smokestack where he could observe results. Presently the

---

irreparably: irreversibly; beyond repair
preposterous: ridiculously foolish
brimful: full to the top
affront: an insult
forecastle: a section of the upper deck of a ship

captain stepped out on the hurricane-deck; next the chief mate appeared; then a clerk. Every moment or two a straggler was added to my audience, and before I got to the head of the island, I had fifteen or twenty people assembled down there under my nose. I began to wonder what the trouble was. As I started across, the captain glanced aloft at me and said, with a sham uneasiness in his voice,

"Where is Mr. Bixby?"

"Gone below, sir."

But that did the business for me. My imagination began to construct dangers out of nothing, and they multiplied faster than I could keep the run of them. All at once I imagined I saw shoal water ahead! The wave of coward agony that surged through me then came near dislocating every joint in me. All my confidence in that crossing vanished. I seized the bell-rope; dropped it, ashamed; seized it again; dropped it once more; clutched it tremblingly once again, and pulled it so feebly that I could hardly hear the stroke myself. Captain and mate sang out instantly, and both together:

"Starboard lead there! And quick about it!"

This was another shock. I began to climb the wheel like a squirrel, but I would hardly get the boat started to port before I would see new dangers on that side, and away I would spin to the other, only to find perils accumulating to starboard and be crazy to get to port again. Then came the leadsman's sepulchral cry:

---

straggler: one who has fallen behind
sham: fake; false; pretended
shoal: shallow
starboard: when looking forward, the right side of a ship
port: when looking forward, the left side of a ship
sepulchral: low and hollow in tone; suggestive of a grave or burial

"D-e-e-p four!"

Deep four in a bottomless crossing! The terror of it took my breath away. "M-a-r-k three! M-a-r-k three! Quarter-less-three! Half twain!"

This was frightful! I seized the bell-ropes and stopped the engines.

"Quarter twain! Quarter twain! *Mark* twain!"

I was helpless. I did not know what in the world to do. I was quaking from head to foot, and I could have hung my hat on my eyes, they stuck out so far.

"Quarter-*less*-twain! Nine-and-a-*half*!"

We were *drawing* nine! My hands were in a nerveless flutter. I could not ring a bell intelligibly with them. I flew to the speaking-tube and shouted to the engineer,

"Oh, Ben, if you love me, back her! Quick, Ben! Oh, back the immortal soul out of her!"

I heard the door close gently. I looked around, and there stood Mr. Bixby, smiling a bland, sweet smile. Then the audience on the hurricane-deck sent up a thundergust of humiliating laughter. I saw it all, now, and felt meaner than the meanest man in human history. I laid in the lead, set the boat in her marks, came ahead on the engines, and said,

"It was a fine trick to play on an orphan, *wasn't* it? I suppose I'll never hear the last of how I was stupid enough to heave the lead at the head of 66."

"Well, no, you won't, maybe. In fact I hope you won't; for I want you to learn something by that experience. Didn't you know there was no bottom in that crossing?"

"Yes, sir, I did."

"Very well, then. You shouldn't have allowed me or

---

meaner: more unworthy; more shameful; more contemptible

anybody else to shake your confidence in that knowledge. Try to remember that. And another thing: when you get into a dangerous place, don't turn coward. That isn't going to help matters any."

It was a good enough lesson, but learned the hard way. Yet about the hardest part of it was that for months I so often had to hear a phrase which I had conceived a particular distaste for. It was, "Oh, Ben, if you love me, back her!"

from

BARRIO BOY
by Ernesto Galarza

*Ernesto Galarza was born in 1905 in the Mexican town of Jalcocotán.
The Mexican Revolution of 1910 compelled his family to immigrate
to the United States, where they eventually settled in Sacramento,
California. Like many other immigrants, they worked on the farms
in the area. Encouraged by one of his teachers, Galarza went on to
attend college, and in time received a doctoral degree from Columbia
University. Galarza became a historian, a professor, and a champion
for the rights of farm workers and other laborers. He told the story
of his early years in* Barrio Boy, *first published in 1971. Galarza
died in 1984.*

My mother and I walked south on Fifth Street one morning
to the corner of Q Street and turned right. Half of the block
was occupied by the Lincoln School. It was a three-story
wooden building, with two wings that gave it the shape of
a double-T connected by a central hall. It was a new building,
painted yellow, with a shingled roof that was not like the red
tile of the school in Mazatlán. I noticed other differences,
none of them very reassuring.

We walked up the wide staircase hand in hand and
through the door, which closed by itself. A mechanical
contraption screwed to the top shut it behind us quietly.

Up to this point the adventure of enrolling me in the school
had been carefully rehearsed. Mrs. Dodson had told us how to

---

barrio: in the United States, a Spanish-speaking neighborhood in a city or town

find it and we had circled it several times on our walks. Friends in the barrio explained that the director was called a principal, and that it was a lady and not a man. They assured us that there was always a person at the school who could speak Spanish.

Exactly as we had been told, there was a sign on the door in both Spanish and English: "Principal." We crossed the hall and entered the office of Miss Nettie Hopley.

Miss Hopley was at a roll-top desk to one side, sitting in a swivel chair that moved on wheels. There was a sofa against the opposite wall, flanked by two windows and a door that opened on a small balcony. Chairs were set around a table and framed pictures hung on the walls of a man with long white hair and another with a sad face and a black beard.

The principal half turned in the swivel chair to look at us over the pinch glasses crossed on the ridge of her nose. To do this she had to duck her head slightly as if she were about to step through a low doorway.

What Miss Hopley said to us we did not know but we saw in her eyes a warm welcome and when she took off her glasses and straightened up she smiled wholeheartedly, like Mrs. Dodson. We were, of course, saying nothing, only catching the friendliness of her voice and the sparkle in her eyes while she said words we did not understand. She signaled us to the table. Almost tiptoeing across the office, I maneuvered myself to keep my mother between me and the gringo lady. In a matter of seconds I had to decide whether she was a possible friend or a menace. We sat down.

maneuvered: moved purposefully
gringo: slang term for a non-Hispanic person, especially American or English
menace: threat

Then Miss Hopley did a formidable thing. She stood up. Had she been standing when we entered she would have seemed tall. But rising from her chair she soared. And what she carried up and up with her was a buxom superstructure, firm shoulders, a straight sharp nose, full cheeks slightly molded by a curved line along the nostrils, thin lips that moved like steel springs, and a high forehead topped by hair gathered in a bun. Miss Hopley was not a giant in body but when she mobilized it to a standing position she seemed a match for giants. I decided I liked her.

She strode to a door in the far corner of the office, opened it and called a name. A boy of about ten years appeared in the doorway. He sat down at one end of the table. He was brown like us, a plump kid with shiny black hair combed straight back, neat, cool, and faintly obnoxious.

Miss Hopley joined us with a large book and some papers in her hand. She, too, sat down and the questions and answers began by way of our interpreter. My name was Ernesto. My mother's name was Henriqueta. My birth certificate was in San Blas. Here was my last report card from the Escuela Municipal Numero 3 para Varones of Mazatlán, and so forth. Miss Hopley put things down in the book and my mother signed a card.

As long as the questions continued, Doña Henriqueta could stay and I was secure. Now that they were over, Miss Hopley saw her to the door, dismissed our interpreter and

---

formidable: extremely impressive; inspiring awe or wonder
buxom: ample; full-figured
superstructure: the upper part of a building or structure
San Blas: a town on the west coast of Mexico
Escuela Municipal Numero 3 para Varones of Mazatlán: Municipal School
    Number 3 for Boys of Mazatlán (a city in western Mexico)
doña: in Spanish, a respectful title for a woman

without further ado took me by the hand and strode down the hall to Miss Ryan's first grade.

Miss Ryan took me to a seat at the front of the room, into which I shrank—the better to survey her. She was, to skinny, somewhat runty me, of a withering height when she patrolled the class. And when I least expected it, there she was, crouching by my desk, her blond radiant face level with mine, her voice patiently maneuvering me over the awful idiocies of the English language.

During the next few weeks Miss Ryan overcame my fears of tall, energetic teachers as she bent over my desk to help me with a word in the pre-primer. Step by step, she loosened me and my classmates from the safe anchorage of the desks for recitations at the blackboard and consultations at her desk. Frequently she burst into happy announcements to the whole class. "Ito can read a sentence," and small Japanese Ito, squint-eyed and shy, slowly read aloud while the class listened in wonder: "Come, Skipper, come. Come and run." The Korean, Portuguese, Italian, and Polish first graders had similar moments of glory, no less shining than mine the day I conquered "butterfly," which I had been persistently pronouncing in standard Spanish as boo-ter-flee. "Children," Miss Ryan called for attention. "Ernesto has learned how to pronounce *butterfly*!" And I proved it with a perfect imitation of Miss Ryan. From that celebrated success, I was soon able to match Ito's progress as a sentence reader with "Come, butterfly, come fly with me."

Like Ito and several other first graders who did not know English, I received private lessons from Miss Ryan in the closet, a narrow hall off the classroom with a door at each end. Next to one of these doors Miss Ryan placed a large chair for herself and a small one for me. Keeping an eye on the class through the open door, she read with me about sheep in the meadow and a frightened chicken going to see the king, coaching me out of my phonetic ruts in words like *pasture, bow-wow-wow, hay,* and *pretty,* which to my Mexican ear and eye had so many unnecessary sounds and letters. She made me watch her lips and then close my eyes as she repeated words I found hard to read. When we came to know each other better, I tried interrupting to tell Miss Ryan how we said it in Spanish. It didn't work. She only said "oh" and went on with *pasture, bow-wow-wow,* and *pretty.* It was as if in that closet we were both discovering together the secrets of the English language and grieving together over the tragedies of Bo-Peep. The main reason I was graduated with honors from the first grade was that I had fallen in love with Miss Ryan. Her radiant, no-nonsense character made us either afraid not to love her or love her so we would not be afraid, I am not sure which. It was not only that we sensed she was with it, but also that she was with us.

Like the first grade, the rest of the Lincoln School was a sampling of the lower part of town where many races made their home. My pals in the second grade were Kazushi, whose parents spoke only Japanese; Matti, a skinny Italian boy; and Manuel, a fat Portuguese who would never get into a fight but wrestled you to the ground and just sat on you. Our assortment of nationalities included Koreans, Yugoslavs, Poles, Irish, and home-grown Americans.

At Lincoln, making us into Americans did not mean scrubbing away what made us originally foreign. The teachers called us as our parents did, or as close as they could pronounce our names in Spanish or Japanese. No

---

phonetic: relating to pronunciation and the sounds of speech

one was ever scolded or punished for speaking in his native tongue on the playground. Matti told the class about his mother's down quilt, which she had made in Italy with the fine feathers of a thousand geese. Encarnación acted out how boys learned to fish in the Philippines. I astounded the third grade with the story of my travels on a stagecoach, which nobody else in the class had seen except in the museum at Sutter's Fort. After a visit to the Crocker Art Gallery and its collection of heroic paintings of the golden age of California, someone showed a silk scroll with a Chinese painting. Miss Hopley herself had a way of expressing wonder over these matters before a class, her eyes wide open until they popped slightly. It was easy for me to feel that becoming a proud American, as she said we should, did not mean feeling ashamed of being a Mexican.

No Gumption

by Russell Baker

For some people, Russell Baker might be most familiar as the host who introduces the televised dramas on Masterpiece Theatre. *Baker was born in Virginia in 1925. After graduating from college in Baltimore, he became a newspaper reporter. Eventually he went on to write for the* New York Times. *In 1979 he was awarded the prestigious Pulitzer Prize for the commentaries he wrote for the* Times. *In 1983 he received a second Pulitzer Prize, this time for his autobiography,* Growing Up, *from which the following excerpt is taken.*

I began working in journalism when I was eight years old. It was my mother's idea. She wanted me to "make something" of myself and, after a level-headed appraisal of my strengths, decided I had better start young if I was to have any chance of keeping up with the competition.

The flaw in my character which she had already spotted was lack of "gumption." My idea of a perfect afternoon was lying in front of the radio rereading my favorite Big Little Book, *Dick Tracy Meets Stooge Viller.* My mother despised inactivity. Seeing me having a good time in repose, she was powerless to hide her disgust. "You've got no more gumption than a bump on a log," she said. "Get out in the kitchen and help Doris do those dirty dishes."

My sister Doris, though two years younger than I, had enough gumption for a dozen people. She positively enjoyed washing dishes, making beds, and cleaning the house. When

---

appraisal: evaluation
gumption: spunk; boldness; initiative

she was only seven she could carry a piece of short-weighted cheese back to the A&P, threaten the manager with legal action, and come back triumphantly with the full quarter-pound we'd paid for and a few ounces extra thrown in for forgiveness. Doris could have made something of herself if she hadn't been a girl. Because of this defect, however, the best she could hope for was a career as a nurse or schoolteacher, the only work that capable females were considered up to in those days.

This must have saddened my mother, this twist of fate that had allocated all the gumption to the daughter and left her with a son who was content with Dick Tracy and Stooge Viller. If disappointed, though, she wasted no energy on self-pity. She would make me make something of myself whether I wanted to or not. "The Lord helps those who help themselves," she said. That was the way her mind worked.

She was realistic about the difficulty. Having sized up the material the Lord had given her to mold, she didn't overestimate what she could do with it. She didn't insist that I grow up to be President of the United States.

Fifty years ago parents still asked boys if they wanted to grow up to be President, and asked it not jokingly but seriously. Many parents who were hardly more than paupers still believed their sons could do it. Abraham Lincoln had done it. We were only sixty-five years from Lincoln. Many a grandfather who walked among us could remember Lincoln's time. Men of grandfatherly age were the worst for asking if you wanted to grow up to be President. A surprising number of little boys said yes and meant it.

---

allocated: distributed; allotted; assigned

I was asked many times myself. No, I would say, I didn't want to grow up to be President. My mother was present during one of these interrogations. An elderly uncle, having posed the usual question and exposed my lack of interest in the Presidency, asked, "Well, what *do* you want to be when you grow up?"

I loved to pick through trash piles and collect empty bottles, tin cans with pretty labels, and discarded magazines. The most desirable job on earth sprang instantly to mind. "I want to be a garbage man," I said.

My uncle smiled, but my mother had seen the first distressing evidence of a bump budding on a log. "Have a little gumption, Russell," she said. Her calling me Russell was a signal of unhappiness. When she approved of me I was always "Buddy."

When I turned eight years old she decided that the job of starting me on the road toward making something of myself could no longer be safely delayed. "Buddy," she said one day, "I want you to come home right after school this afternoon. Somebody's coming and I want you to meet him."

When I burst in that afternoon she was in conference in the parlor with an executive of the Curtis Publishing Company. She introduced me. He bent low from the waist and shook my hand. Was it true as my mother had told him, he asked, that I longed for the opportunity to conquer the world of business?

My mother replied that I was blessed with a rare determination to make something of myself.

"That's right," I whispered.

"But have you got the grit, the character, the never-say-quit spirit it takes to succeed in business?"

---

interrogations: formal questionings
parlor: a room in which guests are received

My mother said I certainly did.

"That's right," I said.

He eyed me silently for a long pause, as though weighing whether I could be trusted to keep his confidence, then spoke man-to-man. Before taking a crucial step, he said, he wanted to advise me that working for the Curtis Publishing Company placed enormous responsibility on a young man. It was one of the great companies of America. Perhaps the greatest publishing house in the world. I had heard, no doubt, of the *Saturday Evening Post*?

Heard of it? My mother said that everyone in our house had heard of the *Saturday Post* and that I, in fact, read it with religious devotion.

Then doubtless, he said, we were also familiar with those two monthly pillars of the magazine world, the *Ladies Home Journal* and the *Country Gentleman*.

Indeed we were familiar with them, said my mother.

Representing the *Saturday Evening Post* was one of the weightiest honors that could be bestowed in the world of business, he said. He was personally proud of being a part of that great corporation.

My mother said he had every right to be.

Again he studied me as though debating whether I was worthy of a knighthood. Finally: "Are you trustworthy?"

My mother said I was the soul of honesty.

"That's right," I said.

The caller smiled for the first time. He told me I was a lucky young man. He admired my spunk. Too many young men thought life was all play. Those young men would not go far in this world. Only a young man willing to work and save

---

crucial: of extreme importance
bestowed: presented as a gift or an honor

25

and keep his face washed and his hair neatly combed could hope to come out on top in a world such as ours. Did I truly and sincerely believe that I was such a young man?

"He certainly does," said my mother.

"That's right," I said.

He said he had been so impressed by what he had seen of me that he was going to make me a representative of the Curtis Publishing Company. On the following Tuesday, he said, thirty freshly printed copies of the *Saturday Evening Post* would be delivered at our door. I would place these magazines, still damp with the ink of the presses, in a handsome canvas bag, sling it over my shoulder, and set forth through the streets to bring the best in journalism, fiction, and cartoons to the American public.

He had brought the canvas bag with him. He presented it with reverence fit for a chasuble. He showed me how to drape the sling over my left shoulder and across the chest so that the pouch lay easily accessible to my right hand, allowing the best in journalism, fiction, and cartoons to be swiftly extracted and sold to a citizenry whose happiness and security depended upon us soldiers of the free press.

The following Tuesday I raced home from school, put the canvas bag over my shoulder, dumped the magazines in, and, tilting to the left to balance their weight on my right hip, embarked on the highway of journalism.

We lived in Belleville, New Jersey, a commuter town at the northern fringe of Newark. It was 1932, the bleakest year of the Depression. My father had died two years before, leaving us with a few pieces of Sears, Roebuck furniture and not much

---

reverence: profound respect
chasuble: a garment worn by a priest
bleakest: gloomiest; most hopeless

else, and my mother had taken Doris and me to live with one of her younger brothers. This was my Uncle Allen. Uncle Allen had made something of himself by 1932. As salesman for a soft-drink bottler in Newark, he had an income of $30 a week; wore pearl-gray spats, detachable collars, and a three-piece suit; was happily married; and took in threadbare relatives.

With my load of magazines I headed toward Belleville Avenue. That's where the people were. There were two filling stations at the intersection with Union Avenue, as well as an A&P, a fruit stand, a bakery, a barber shop, Zuccarelli's drugstore, and a diner shaped like a railroad car. For several hours I made myself highly visible, shifting position now and then from corner to corner, from shop window to shop window, to make sure everyone could see the heavy black lettering on the canvas bag that said *The Saturday Evening Post*. When the angle of the light indicated it was suppertime, I walked back to the house.

"How many did you sell, Buddy?" my mother asked.

"None."

"Where did you go?"

"The corner of Belleville and Union Avenues."

"What did you do?"

"Stood on the corner waiting for somebody to buy a *Saturday Evening Post.*"

"You just stood there?"

"Didn't sell a single one."

"For God's sake, Russell!"

Uncle Allen intervened. "I've been thinking about it for some time," he said, "and I've about decided to take the *Post* regularly. Put me down as a regular customer." I handed him

---

spats: once-fashionable pieces of cloth or leather worn over the tops of shoes

a magazine and he paid me a nickel. It was the first nickel I earned.

Afterwards my mother instructed me in salesmanship. I would have to ring doorbells, address adults with charming self-confidence, and break down resistance with a sales talk pointing out that no one, no matter how poor, could afford to be without the *Saturday Evening Post* in the home.

I told my mother I'd changed my mind about wanting to succeed in the magazine business.

"If you think I'm going to raise a good-for-nothing," she replied, "you've got another thing coming." She told me to hit the streets with the canvas bag and start ringing doorbells the instant school was out next day. When I objected that I didn't feel any aptitude for salesmanship, she asked how I'd like to lend her my leather belt so she could whack some sense into me. I bowed to superior will and entered journalism with a heavy heart.

My mother and I had fought this battle almost as long as I could remember. It probably started even before memory began, when I was a country child in northern Virginia and my mother, dissatisfied with my father's plain workman's life, determined that I would not grow up like him and his people, with calluses on their hands, overalls on their backs, and fourth-grade educations in their heads. She had fancier ideas of life's possibilities. Introducing me to the *Saturday Evening Post*, she was trying to wean me as early as possible from my father's world where men left with lunch pails at sunup, worked with their hands until the grime ate into the pores, and died with a few sticks of mail-order furniture as their legacy.

---

wean: gradually to detach or remove from
legacy: property left in a will

In my mother's vision of the better life there were desks and white collars, well-pressed suits, evenings of reading and lively talk, and perhaps—if a man were very, very lucky and hit the jackpot, really made something important of himself—perhaps there might be a fantastic salary of $5,000 a year to support a big house and a Buick with a rumble seat and a vacation in Atlantic City.

And so I set forth with my sack of magazines. I was afraid of the dogs that snarled behind the doors of potential buyers. I was timid about ringing the doorbells of strangers, relieved when no one came to the door, and scared when someone did. Despite my mother's instructions, I could not deliver an engaging sales pitch. When a door opened I simply asked, "Want to buy a *Saturday Evening Post*?" In Belleville few persons did. It was a town of 30,000 people, and most weeks I rang a fair majority of its doorbells. But I rarely sold my thirty copies. Some weeks I canvassed the entire town for six days and still had four or five unsold magazines on Monday evening; then I dreaded the coming of Tuesday morning, when a batch of thirty fresh *Saturday Evening Posts* was due at the front door.

"Better get out there and sell the rest of those magazines tonight," my mother would say.

I usually posted myself then at a busy intersection where a traffic light controlled commuter flow from Newark. When the light turned red I stood on the curb and shouted my sales pitch at the motorists.

"Want to buy a *Saturday Evening Post*?"

---

rumble seat: in the back of early model cars, an open seat that could be folded down

canvassed: went through an area or to people to get their support, business, vote, etc.

One rainy night when car windows were sealed against me I came back soaked and with not a single sale to report. My mother beckoned to Doris.

"Go back down there with Buddy and show him how to sell these magazines," she said.

Brimming with zest, Doris, who was then seven years old, returned with me to the corner. She took a magazine from the bag, and when the light turned red she strode to the nearest car and banged her small fist against the closed window. The driver, probably startled at what he took to be a midget assaulting his car, lowered the window to stare, and Doris thrust a *Saturday Evening Post* at him.

"You need this magazine," she piped, "and it only costs a nickel."

Her salesmanship was irresistible. Before the light changed half a dozen times she disposed of the entire batch. I didn't feel humiliated. To the contrary. I was so happy I decided to give her a treat. Leading her to the vegetable store on Belleville Avenue, I bought three apples, which cost a nickel, and gave her one.

"You shouldn't waste money," she said.

"Eat your apple." I bit into mine.

"You shouldn't eat before supper," she said. "It'll spoil your appetite."

Back at the house that evening, she dutifully reported me for wasting a nickel. Instead of a scolding, I was rewarded with a pat on the back for having the good sense to buy fruit instead of candy. My mother reached into her bottomless supply of maxims and told Doris, "An apple a day keeps the doctor away."

---

zest: gusto; enthusiasm; spirit
maxims: proverbs; sayings packed with wisdom or advice

By the time I was ten I had learned all my mother's maxims by heart. Asking to stay up past normal bedtime, I knew that a refusal would be explained with, "Early to bed and early to rise, makes a man healthy, wealthy, and wise." If I whimpered about having to get up early in the morning, I could depend on her to say, "The early bird gets the worm."

The one I most despised was, "If at first you don't succeed, try, try again." This was the battle cry with which she constantly sent me back into the hopeless struggle whenever I moaned that I had rung every doorbell in town and knew there wasn't a single potential buyer left in Belleville that week. After listening to my explanation, she handed me the canvas bag and said, "If at first you don't succeed..."

Three years in that job, which I would gladly have quit after the first day except for her insistence, produced at least one valuable result. My mother finally concluded that I would never make something of myself by pursuing a life in business and started considering careers that demanded less competitive zeal.

One evening when I was eleven I brought home a short "composition" on my summer vacation which the teacher had graded with an A. Reading it with her own school-teacher's eye, my mother agreed that it was top-drawer seventh grade prose and complimented me. Nothing more was said about it immediately, but a new idea had taken life in her mind. Halfway through supper she suddenly interrupted the conversation.

"Buddy," she said, "maybe you could be a writer."

I clasped the idea to my heart. I had never met a writer, had shown no previous urge to write, and hadn't a notion

zeal: eagerness; intense passion to achieve some goal or advance some cause

how to become a writer, but I loved stories and thought that making up stories must surely be almost as much fun as reading them. Best of all, though, and what really gladdened my heart, was the ease of the writer's life. Writers did not have to trudge through the town peddling from canvas bags, defending themselves against angry dogs, being rejected by surly strangers. Writers did not have to ring doorbells. So far as I could make out, what writers did couldn't even be classified as work.

I was enchanted. Writers didn't have to have any gumption at all. I did not dare tell anybody for fear of being laughed at in the schoolyard, but secretly I decided that what I'd like to be when I grew up was a writer.

from

I KNOW WHY THE
CAGED BIRD SINGS
by Maya Angelou

On April 4, 1928, Maya Angelou was born Marguerite Johnson in St. Louis, Missouri. The name "Maya" came from her little brother, Bailey, who called her "mya sister." Angelou is a poet, author, playwright, dancer, performer, film producer and director, and champion of civil rights. In 1992, she was honored by being asked to read an original poem at the inauguration of Bill Clinton as president.

In I Know Why the Caged Bird Sings, *Angelou tells the story of her life up to the age of sixteen. The book is the first in a series of autobiographical works.*

When I was three and Bailey four, we had arrived in the musty little town, wearing tags on our wrists which instructed—"To Whom It May Concern"—that we were Marguerite and Bailey Johnson Jr., from Long Beach, California, en route to Stamps, Arkansas, c/o Mrs. Annie Henderson.

Our parents had decided to put an end to their calamitous marriage, and Father shipped us home to his mother. A porter had been charged with our welfare—he got off the train the next day in Arizona—and our tickets were pinned to my brother's inside coat pocket.

---

en route: on the way
c/o: care of
calamitous: disastrous; causing great distress or misery

I don't remember much of the trip, but after we reached the segregated southern part of the journey, things must have looked up. Negro passengers, who always traveled with loaded lunch boxes, felt sorry for "the poor little motherless darlings" and plied us with cold fried chicken and potato salad.

Years later I discovered that the United States had been crossed thousands of times by frightened Black children traveling alone to their newly affluent parents in Northern cities, or back to grandmothers in Southern towns when the urban North reneged on its economic promises.

The town reacted to us as its inhabitants had reacted to all things new before our coming. It regarded us a while without curiosity but with caution, and after we were seen to be harmless (and children) it closed in around us, as a real mother embraces a stranger's child. Warmly, but not too familiarly.

We lived with our grandmother and uncle in the rear of the Store (it was always spoken of with a capital s), which she had owned some twenty-five years.

Early in the century, Momma (we soon stopped calling her Grandmother) sold lunches to the sawmen in the lumberyard (east Stamps) and the seedmen at the cotton gin (west Stamps). Her crisp meat pies and cool lemonade, when joined to her miraculous ability to be in two places at the same time, assured her business success. From being a mobile lunch counter, she set up a stand between the two points of fiscal interest and supplied the workers' needs for

---

affluent: wealthy
reneged: failed to fulfill a promise
fiscal: relating to financial matters

a few years. Then she had the Store built in the heart of the Negro area. Over the years it became the lay center of activities in town. On Saturdays, barbers sat their customers in the shade on the porch of the Store, and troubadours on their ceaseless crawlings through the South leaned across its benches and sang their sad songs of The Brazos while they played juice harps and cigar-box guitars.

The formal name of the Store was the Wm. Johnson General Merchandise Store. Customers could find food staples, a good variety of colored thread, mash for hogs, corn for chickens, coal oil for lamps, light bulbs for the wealthy, shoestrings, hair dressing, balloons, and flower seeds. Anything not visible had only to be ordered.

Until we became familiar enough to belong to the Store and it to us, we were locked up in a Fun House of Things where the attendant had gone home for life.

Each year I watched the field across from the Store turn caterpillar green, then gradually frosty white. I knew exactly how long it would be before the big wagons would pull into the front yard and load on the cotton pickers at daybreak to carry them to the remains of slavery's plantations.

During the picking season my grandmother would get out of bed at four o'clock (she never used an alarm clock) and creak down to her knees and chant in a sleep-filled voice, "Our Father, thank you for letting me see this New Day. Thank you that you didn't allow the bed I lay on last night to be my cooling board,

---

lay: unrelated to church matters
troubadours: traveling singers
The Brazos: region in central Texas near the Brazos River
juice harps: musical instruments held between the teeth and plucked to play
mash: grain mixture used to feed farm animals

nor my blanket my winding sheet. Guide my feet this day along the straight and narrow, and help me to put a bridle on my tongue. Bless this house, and everybody in it. Thank you, in the name of your Son, Jesus Christ, Amen."

Before she had quite arisen, she called our names and issued orders, and pushed her large feet into homemade slippers and across the bare lye-washed wooden floor to light the coal-oil lamp.

The lamplight in the Store gave a soft make-believe feeling to our world which made me want to whisper and walk about on tiptoe. The odors of onions and oranges and kerosene had been mixing all night and wouldn't be disturbed until the wooded slat was removed from the door and the early morning air forced its way in with the bodies of people who had walked miles to reach the pickup place.

"Sister, I'll have two cans of sardines."

"I'm gonna work so fast today I'm gonna make you look like you standing still."

"Lemme have a hunk uh cheese and some sody crackers."

"Just gimme a coupla them fat peanut paddies." That would be from a picker who was taking his lunch. The greasy brown paper sack was stuck behind the bib of his overalls. He'd use the candy as a snack before the noon sun called the workers to rest.

In those tender mornings the Store was full of laughing, joking, boasting and bragging. One man was going to pick two hundred pounds of cotton, and another three hundred. Even the children were promising to bring home fo' bits and six bits.

The champion picker of the day before was the hero of the dawn. If he prophesied that the cotton in today's field

---

prophesied: predicted

was going to be sparse and stick to the bolls like glue, every listener would grunt a hearty agreement.

The sound of the empty cotton sacks dragging over the floor and the murmurs of waking people were sliced by the cash register as we rang up the five-cent sales.

If the morning sounds and smells were touched with the supernatural, the late afternoon had all the features of the normal Arkansas life. In the dying sunlight the people dragged, rather than their empty cotton sacks.

Brought back to the Store, the pickers would step out of the backs of trucks and fold down, dirt-disappointed, to the ground. No matter how much they had picked, it wasn't enough. Their wages wouldn't even get them out of debt to my grandmother, not to mention the staggering bill that waited on them at the white commissary downtown....

During these years in Stamps, I met and fell in love with William Shakespeare. He was my first white love. Although I enjoyed and respected Kipling, Poe, Butler, Thackeray and Henley, I saved my young and loyal passion for Paul Lawrence Dunbar, Langston Hughes, James Weldon Johnson and W.E.B. Du Bois' "Litany at Atlanta." But it was Shakespeare who said, "When in disgrace with fortune and men's eyes." It was a state with which I felt myself most familiar. I pacified myself about his whiteness by saying that after all he had been dead so long it couldn't matter to anyone any more.

---

bolls: seed-bearing pods of cotton plants
commissary: a store that sells food, equipment, and supplies
pacified: soothed; calmed; put at peace

Bailey and I decided to memorize a scene from *The Merchant of Venice*, but we realized that Momma would question us about the author and that we'd have to tell her that Shakespeare was white, and it wouldn't matter to her whether he was dead or not. So we chose "The Creation" by James Weldon Johnson instead….

Weighing the half-pounds of flour, excluding the scoop, and depositing them dust-free into the thin paper sacks held a simple kind of adventure for me. I developed an eye for measuring how full a silver-looking ladle of flour, mash, meal, sugar or corn had to be to push the scale indicator over to eight ounces or one pound. When I was absolutely accurate our appreciative customers used to admire: "Sister Henderson sure got some smart grandchildrens." If I was off in the Store's favor, the eagle-eyed women would say, "Put some more in that sack, child. Don't you try to make your profit offa me."

Then I would quietly but persistently punish myself. For every bad judgment, the fine was no silver-wrapped Kisses, the sweet chocolate drops that I loved more than anything in the world, except Bailey. And maybe canned pineapples. My obsession with pineapples nearly drove me mad. I dreamt of the days when I would be grown and able to buy a whole carton for myself alone.

Although the syrupy golden rings sat in their exotic cans on our shelves year round, we only tasted them during Christmas. Momma used the juice to make almost-black fruit cakes. Then she lined heavy soot-encrusted iron skillets with the pineapple rings for rich upside-down cakes. Bailey and

---

The Merchant of Venice: one of Shakepeare's plays
"The Creation" by James Weldon Johnson: See page 68 in this book.
exotic: of foreign origin; exciting because unusual or strange

I received one slice each, and I carried mine around for hours, shredding off the fruit until nothing was left except the perfume on my fingers. I'd like to think that my desire for pineapples was so sacred that I wouldn't allow myself to steal a can (which was possible) and eat it alone out in the garden, but I'm certain that I must have weighed the possibility of the scent exposing me and didn't have the nerve to attempt it.

Until I was thirteen and left Arkansas for good, the Store was my favorite place to be. Alone and empty in the mornings, it looked like an unopened present from a stranger. Opening the front doors was pulling the ribbon off the unexpected gift. The light would come in softly (we faced north), easing itself over the shelves of mackerel, salmon, tobacco, thread. It fell flat on the big vat of lard and by noontime during the summer the grease had softened to a thick soup. Whenever I walked into the Store in the afternoon, I sensed that it was tired. I alone could hear the slow pulse of its job half done. But just before bedtime, after numerous people had walked in and out, had argued over their bills, or joked about their neighbors, or just dropped in "to give Sister Henderson a 'Hi y'all,'" the promise of magic mornings returned to the Store and spread itself over the family in washed life waves....

[Marguerite's mother comes to Stamps, and she takes Marguerite away with her for a visit to St. Louis. At about the age of ten, Marguerite returns to Stamps, withdrawn and silent.]

For nearly a year, I sopped around the house, the Store, the school and the church, like an old biscuit, dirty and inedible.

---

inedible: impossible to eat

Then I met, or rather got to know, the lady who threw me my first life line.

Mrs. Bertha Flowers was the aristocrat of Black Stamps. She had the grace of control to appear warm in the coldest weather, and on the Arkansas summer days it seemed she had a private breeze which swirled around, cooling her. She was thin without the taut look of wiry people, and her printed voile dresses and flowered hats were as right for her as denim overalls for a farmer. She was our side's answer to the richest white woman in town.

Her skin was a rich black that would have peeled like a plum if snagged, but then no one would have thought of getting close enough to Mrs. Flowers to ruffle her dress, let alone snag her skin. She didn't encourage familiarity. She wore gloves too.

I don't think I ever saw Mrs. Flowers laugh, but she smiled often. A slow widening of her thin black lips to show even, small white teeth, then the slow effortless closing. When she chose to smile on me, I always wanted to thank her. The action was so graceful and inclusively benign.

She was one of the few gentlewomen I have ever known, and has remained throughout my life the measure of what a human being can be.

Momma had a strange relationship with her. Most often when she passed on the road in front of the Store, she spoke to Momma in that soft yet carrying voice, "Good day, Mrs. Henderson." Momma responded with "How you, Sister Flowers?"

---

aristocrat: person of high social class or status
taut: pulled tight
voile: lightweight fabric made from cotton
benign: kind; pleasant; gentle

Mrs. Flowers didn't belong to our church, nor was she Momma's familiar. Why on earth did she insist on calling her Sister Flowers? Shame made me want to hide my face. Mrs. Flowers deserved better than to be called Sister. Then, Momma left out the verb. Why not ask, "How are you, Mrs. Flowers?" With the unbalanced passion of the young, I hated her for showing her ignorance to Mrs. Flowers. It didn't occur to me for many years that they were as alike as sisters, separated only by formal education.

Although I was upset, neither of the women was in the least shaken by what I thought an unceremonious greeting. Mrs. Flowers would continue her easy gait up the hill to her little bungalow, and Momma kept on shelling peas or doing whatever had brought her to the front porch.

Occasionally, though, Mrs. Flowers would drift off the road and down to the Store and Momma would say to me, "Sister, you go on and play." As I left I would hear the beginning of an intimate conversation. Momma persistently using the wrong verb, or none at all.

"Brother and Sister Wilcox is sho'ly the meanest—" "Is" Momma? "Is"? Oh, please, not "is," Momma, for two or more. But they talked, and from the side of the building where I waited for the ground to open up and swallow me, I heard the soft-voiced Mrs. Flowers and the textured voice of my grandmother merging and melting. They were interrupted from time to time by giggles that must have come from Mrs. Flowers (Momma never giggled in her life). Then she was gone….

One summer afternoon, sweet-milk fresh in my memory, she stopped at the Store to buy provisions. Another Negro

gait: manner of walking
provisions: supplies

woman of her health and age would have been expected to carry the paper sacks home in one hand, but Momma said, "Sister Flowers, I'll send Bailey up to your house with these things."

She smiled that slow dragging smile, "Thank you, Mrs. Henderson. I'd prefer Marguerite, though." My name was beautiful when she said it. "I've been meaning to talk to her, anyway." They gave each other age-group looks.

Momma said, "Well, that's all right then. Sister, go and change your dress. You going to Sister Flowers's."

The chifforobe was a maze. What on earth did one put on to go to Mrs. Flowers' house? I knew I shouldn't put on a Sunday dress. It might be sacrilegious. Certainly not a house dress, since I was already wearing a fresh one. I chose a school dress, naturally. It was formal without suggesting that going to Mrs. Flowers' house was equivalent to attending church.

I trusted myself back into the Store.

"Now, don't you look nice." I had chosen the right thing, for once.

"Mrs. Henderson, you make most of the children's clothes, don't you?"

"Yes, ma'am. Sure do. Store-bought clothes ain't hardly worth the thread it take to stitch them."

"I'll say you do a lovely job, though, so neat. That dress looks professional."

Momma was enjoying the seldom-received compliments. Since everyone we knew (except Mrs. Flowers, of course) could sew competently, praise was rarely handed out for the commonly practiced craft.

---

chifforobe: a piece of furniture often with drawers on one side and space for hanging clothes on the other

"I try, with the help of the Lord, Sister Flowers, to finish the inside just like I does the outside. Come here, Sister."

I had buttoned up the collar and tied the belt, apron-like, in back. Momma told me to turn around. With one hand she pulled the strings and the belt fell free at both sides of my waist. Then her large hands were at my neck, opening the button loops. I was terrified. What was happening?

"Take it off, Sister." She had her hands on the hem of the dress.

"I don't need to see the inside, Mrs. Henderson, I can tell..." But the dress was over my head and my arms were stuck in the sleeves. Momma said, "That'll do. See here, Sister Flowers, I French-seams around the armholes." Through the cloth film, I saw the shadow approach. "That makes it last longer. Children these days would bust out of sheet-metal clothes. They so rough."

"That is a very good job, Mrs. Henderson. You should be proud. You can put your dress back on, Marguerite."

"No ma'am. Pride is a sin. And 'cording to the Good Book, it goeth before a fall."

"That's right. So the Bible says. It's a good thing to keep in mind."

I wouldn't look at either of them. Momma hadn't thought that taking off my dress in front of Mrs. Flowers would kill me stone dead. If I had refused, she would have thought I was trying to be "womanish" and might have remembered St. Louis. Mrs. Flowers had known that I would be embarrassed and that was even worse. I picked up the groceries and went out to wait in the hot sunshine. It would be fitting if I got a sunstroke and died before they came outside. Just dropped dead on the slanting porch.

There was a little path beside the rocky road, and Mrs. Flowers walked in front swinging her arms and picking her way over the stones.

She said, without turning her head, to me, "I hear you're doing very good school work, Marguerite, but that it's all written. The teachers report that they have trouble getting you to talk in class." We passed the triangular farm on our left and the path widened to allow us to walk together. I hung back in the separate unasked and unanswerable questions.

"Come and walk along with me, Marguerite." I couldn't have refused even if I wanted to. She pronounced my name so nicely. Or more correctly, she spoke each word with such clarity that I was certain a foreigner who didn't understand English could have understood her.

"Now no one is going to make you talk—possibly no one can. But bear in mind, language is man's way of communicating with his fellow man and it is language alone which separates him from the lower animals." That was a totally new idea to me, and I would need time to think about it.

"Your grandmother says you read a lot. Every chance you get. That's good, but not good enough. Words mean more than what is set down on paper. It takes the human voice to infuse them with the shades of deeper meaning."

I memorized the part about the human voice infusing words. It seemed so valid and poetic.

She said she was going to give me some books and that I not only must read them, I must read them aloud. She suggested that I try to make a sentence sound in as many different ways as possible.

"I'll accept no excuse if you return a book to me that has been badly handled." My imagination boggled at the

---

boggled: hesitated in fear, doubt, or amazement

punishment I would deserve if in fact I did abuse a book of Mrs. Flowers'. Death would be too kind and brief.

The odors in the house surprised me. Somehow I had never connected Mrs. Flowers with food or eating or any other common experience of common people. There must have been an outhouse, too, but my mind never recorded it.

The sweet scent of vanilla had met us as she opened the door.

"I made tea cookies this morning. You see, I had planned to invite you for cookies and lemonade so we could have this little chat. The lemonade is in the icebox."

It followed that Mrs. Flowers would have ice on an ordinary day, when most families in our town bought ice late on Saturdays only a few times during the summer to be used in the wooden ice-cream freezers.

She took the bags from me and disappeared through the kitchen door. I looked around the room that I had never in my wildest fantasies imagined I would see. Browned photographs leered or threatened from the walls and the white, freshly done curtains pushed against themselves and against the wind. I wanted to gobble up the room entire and take it to Bailey, who would help me analyze and enjoy it.

"Have a seat, Marguerite. Over there by the table." She carried a platter covered with a tea towel. Although she warned that she hadn't tried her hand at baking sweets for some time, I was certain that like everything else about her the cookies would be perfect.

They were flat round wafers, slightly browned on the edges and butter-yellow in the center. With the cold lemonade they were sufficient for childhood's lifelong diet. Remembering my manners, I took nice little lady-like bites off the edges. She said she had made them expressly for me and that she had a few in the kitchen that I could take home to my brother. So I jammed one whole cake in my mouth and the rough crumbs scratched the insides of my jaws, and if I hadn't had to swallow, it would have been a dream come true.

As I ate she began the first of what we later called "my lessons in living." She said that I must always be intolerant of ignorance but understanding of illiteracy. That some people, unable to go to school, were more educated and even more intelligent than college professors. She encouraged me to listen carefully to what country people called mother wit. That in those homely sayings was couched the collective wisdom of generations.

When I finished the cookies she brushed off the table and brought a thick, small book from the bookcase. I had read *A Tale of Two Cities* and found it up to my standards as a romantic novel. She opened the first page and I heard poetry for the first time in my life.

"It was the best of times and the worst of times..." Her voice slid in and curved down through and over the words. She was nearly singing. I wanted to look at the pages. Were they the same that I had read? Or were there notes, music, lined on the pages, as in a hymn book? Her sounds began cascading gently. I knew from listening to a thousand preachers that she was nearing the end of her reading, and I hadn't really heard, heard to understand, a single word.

"How do you like that?"

A Tale of Two Cities: a historical novel by the English novelist Charles Dickens, published in 1859, and set in the time of the French Revolution
cascading: pouring down like a waterfall

It occurred to me that she expected a response. The sweet vanilla flavor was still on my tongue and her reading was a wonder in my ears. I had to speak.

I said, "Yes, ma'am." It was the least I could do, but it was the most also.

"There's one more thing. Take this book of poems and memorize one for me. Next time you pay me a visit, I want you to recite."

I have tried often to search behind the sophistication of years for the enchantment I so easily found in those gifts. The essence escapes but its aura remains. To be allowed, no, invited, into the private lives of strangers, and to share their joys and fears, was a chance to exchange the Southern bitter wormwood for a cup of mead with Beowulf or a hot cup of tea and milk with Oliver Twist. When I said aloud, "It is a far, far better thing that I do, than I have ever done..." tears of love filled my eyes at my selflessness.

On that first day, I ran down the hill and into the road (few cars ever came along it) and had the good sense to stop running before I reached the Store.

I was liked, and what a difference it made. I was respected not as Mrs. Henderson's grandchild or Bailey's sister but for just being Marguerite Johnson.

Childhood's logic never asks to be proved (all conclusions are absolute). I didn't question why Mrs. Flowers had

---

aura: an invisible breath, glow, or presence
wormwood: a bitter-tasting plant; anything harsh or bitter
mead: a wine made from fermented honey and water
Beowulf: the hero of an epic poem dating from about the eighth century
Oliver Twist: the main character in *Oliver Twist*, a novel by Charles
    Dickens, published in 1837–38
"It is a far, far better thing...": a famous quotation from the ending of
    A Tale of Two Cities

singled me out for attention, nor did it occur to me that Momma might have asked her to give me a little talking to. All I cared about was that she had made tea cookies for *me* and read to *me* from her favorite book. It was enough to prove that she liked me.

STORIES IN VERSE

LOCHINVAR
by Sir Walter Scott

Oh, young Lochinvar is come out of the West;
Through all the wide Border his steed was the best;
And save his good broadsword he weapons had none;
He rode all unarmed, and he rode all alone.
So faithful in love, and so dauntless in war,
There never was knight like the young Lochinvar.

He stayed not for brake, and he stopped not for stone;
He swam the Eske river where ford there was none;
But, ere he alighted at Netherby gate,
The bride had consented, the gallant came late:
For a laggard in love, and a dastard in war,
Was to wed the fair Ellen of brave Lochinvar.

So boldly he entered the Netherby hall,
'Mong bridesmen and kinsmen, and brothers and all.
Then spoke the bride's father, his hand on his sword
(For the poor craven bridegroom said never a word),
"Oh! come ye in peace here, or come ye in war,
Or to dance at our bridal, young Lord Lochinvar?"

---

save: except
dauntless: fearless
brake: dense marshland
ford: a shallow place in a body or water
alighted: dismounted from a horse; got down from something
laggard: someone who is slow to act
dastard: a coward; a sneaky person
craven: cowardly

"I long wooed your daughter, my suit you denied.
Love swells like the Solway, but ebbs like its tide;
And now am I come, with this lost love of mine
To lead but one measure, drink one cup of wine.
There are maidens in Scotland more lovely by far,
That would gladly be bride to the young Lochinvar."

The bride kissed the goblet; the knight took it up:
He quaffed off the wine, and he threw down the cup.
She looked down to blush, and she looked up to sigh,
With a smile on her lips and a tear in her eye.
He took her soft hand ere her mother could bar,—
"Now tread we a measure!" said young Lochinvar.

So stately his form, and so lovely her face,
That never a hall such a galliard did grace;
While her mother did fret, and her father did fume,
And the bridegroom stood dangling his bonnet and plume;
And the bride-maidens whispered "'Twere better by far
To have matched our fair cousin with young Lochinvar."

Solway: an inlet of the Irish Sea, between England and Scotland
ebbs: decreases; goes out like the tide
quaffed: drank
tread a measure: dance
galliard: a lively dance

One touch to her hand, and one word in her ear,
When they reached the hall door, and the charger stood near;
So light to the croupe the fair lady he swung,
So light to the saddle before her he sprung!
"She is won! we are gone, over bank, bush, and scaur!
They'll have fleet steeds that follow!" quoth young Lochinvar.

There was mounting 'mong Graemes of the Netherby clan;
Forsters, Fenwicks, and Musgraves, they rode and they ran;
There was racing and chasing on Cannobie Lee;
But the lost bride of Netherby ne'er did they see.
So daring in love, and so dauntless in war,
Have ye e'er heard of gallant like young Lochinvar?

---

charger: a horse for battle
croupe (also spelled *croup*): hind end
scaur: a steep, rocky bank

THE RAVEN
by Edgar Allan Poe

Once upon a midnight dreary, while I pondered, weak and weary,
Over many a quaint and curious volume of forgotten lore—
While I nodded, nearly napping, suddenly there came a tapping,
As of some one gently rapping, rapping at my chamber door.
"'Tis some visitor," I muttered, "tapping at my chamber door—
Only this and nothing more."

Ah, distinctly I remember it was in the bleak December,
And each separate dying ember wrought its ghost upon the floor.
Eagerly I wished the morrow; —vainly I had sought to borrow
From my books surcease of sorrow—sorrow for the lost Lenore—
For the rare and radiant maiden whom the angels name Lenore—
Nameless here for evermore.

And the silken sad uncertain rustling of each purple curtain
Thrilled me—filled me with fantastic terrors never felt before;
So that now, to still the beating of my heart, I stood repeating
"'Tis some visitor entreating entrance at my chamber door—
Some late visitor entreating entrance at my chamber door;
This it is and nothing more."

---

quaint: unusual
lore: learning; body of knowledge
surcease: an end
fantastic: unreal; from one's fancy or imagination
entreating: pleading; begging

Presently my soul grew stronger; hesitating then no longer,
"Sir," said I, "or Madam, truly your forgiveness I implore;
But the fact is I was napping, and so gently you came rapping,
And so faintly you came tapping, tapping at my chamber door,
That I scarce was sure I heard you"—here I opened wide the door;—
                    Darkness there and nothing more.

Deep into that darkness peering, long I stood there wondering, fearing,
Doubting, dreaming dreams no mortal ever dared to dream before;
But the silence was unbroken, and the stillness gave no token,
And the only word there spoken was the whispered word, "Lenore!"
This I whispered, and an echo murmured back the word, "Lenore!"
                    Merely this and nothing more.

Back into the chamber turning, all my soul within me burning,
Soon again I heard a tapping something louder than before.
"Surely," said I, "surely that is something at my window lattice;
Let me see, then, what thereat is, and this mystery explore—
Let my heart be still a moment and this mystery explore; —
                    'Tis the wind and nothing more!"

---

token: a sign or clue
lattice: the crossed wood or metal frame over the glass of a window
thereat: at that place

Open here I flung the shutter, when, with many a flirt and flutter,
In there stepped a stately Raven of the saintly days of yore.
Not the least obeisance made he; not a minute stopped or stayed he;
But, with mien of lord or lady, perched above my chamber door—
Perched upon a bust of Pallas just above my chamber door—
                         Perched, and sat, and nothing more.

Then this ebony bird beguiling my sad fancy into smiling,
By the grave and stern decorum of the countenance it wore,
"Though thy crest be shorn and shaven, thou," I said, "art sure
        no craven,
Ghastly grim and ancient Raven wandering from the Nightly shore—
Tell me what thy lordly name is on the Night's Plutonian shore!"
                         Quoth the Raven, "Nevermore."

Much I marveled this ungainly fowl to hear discourse so plainly,
Though its answer little meaning—little relevancy bore;
For we cannot help agreeing that no living human being
Ever yet was blessed with seeing bird above his chamber door—
Bird or beast upon the sculptured bust above his chamber door,
                         With such name as "Nevermore."

---

flirt: sudden movement
yore: long ago
obeisance: a show of respect
mien: bearing; attitude; appearance
Pallas: a name for Athena, the Greek goddess of wisdom
beguiling: deceiving; charming through deceptive means
fancy: imagination
countenance: expression
craven: a coward
Plutonian: having to do with the underworld, which the ancient Romans believed
    to be ruled by the god Pluto
quoth: said
discourse: talk; converse

But the Raven, sitting lonely on that placid bust, spoke only
That one word, as if his soul in that one word he did outpour.
Nothing further then he uttered—not a feather then he fluttered—
Till I scarcely more than muttered, "Other friends have flown before—
On the morrow *he* will leave me, as my Hopes have flown before."
                    Then the bird said, "Nevermore."

Startled at the stillness broken by reply so aptly spoken,
"Doubtless," said I, "what it utters is its only stock and store
Caught from some unhappy master whom unmerciful Disaster
Followed fast and followed faster till his songs one burden bore—
Till the dirges of his Hope that melancholy burden bore
                    Of 'Never—nevermore.'"

But the Raven still beguiling all my sad soul into smiling,
Straight I wheeled a cushioned seat in front of bird and bust and door;
Then, upon the velvet sinking, I betook myself to linking
Fancy unto fancy, thinking what this ominous bird of yore—
What this grim, ungainly, ghastly, gaunt, and ominous bird of yore
                    Meant in croaking "Nevermore."

This I sat engaged in guessing, but no syllable expressing
To the fowl whose fiery eyes now burned into my bosom's core;
This and more I sat divining, with my head at ease reclining
On the cushion's velvet lining that the lamp-light gloated o'er,
But whose velvet violet lining with the lamp-light gloating o'er,
                    She shall press, ah, nevermore!

placid: calm; serene
dirges: slow, sad songs of grief
ominous: threatening; foreboding
divining: figuring out; guessing

Then, methought, the air grew denser, perfumed from an unseen
    censer
Swung by Seraphim whose foot-falls tinkled on the tufted floor.
"Wretch," I cried, "thy God hath lent thee—by these angels he
    hath sent thee
Respite—respite and nepenthe from thy memories of Lenore;
Quaff, oh, quaff this kind nepenthe and forget this lost Lenore!"
                Quoth the Raven, "Nevermore."

"Prophet!" said I, "thing of evil! —prophet still, if bird or devil! —
Whether Tempter sent, or whether tempest tossed thee here ashore,
Desolate yet all undaunted, on this desert land enchanted—
On this home by Horror haunted—tell me truly, I implore—
Is there—is there balm in Gilead? —tell me—tell me, I implore!"
                Quoth the Raven, "Nevermore."

"Prophet!" said I, "thing of evil! —prophet still, if bird or devil!
By that Heaven that bends above us—by that God we both adore—
Tell this soul with sorrow laden if, within the distant Aidenn,
It shall clasp a sainted maiden whom the angels name Lenore—
Clasp a rare and radiant maiden whom the angels name Lenore."
                Quoth the Raven, "Nevermore."

---

censer: container in which incense is burned, usually during a religious ritual
Seraphim: angels
respite: period of rest or relief
nepenthe: liquid used in ancient times to cause forgetfulness of one's grief
quaff: to drink
tempest: a storm
undaunted: unafraid; not discouraged
balm in Gilead: a healing ointment mentioned in the Bible
Aidenn: Eden, or paradise

"Be that word our sign of parting, bird or fiend!" I shrieked,
    upstarting—
"Get thee back into the tempest and the Night's Plutonian shore!
Leave no black plume as a token of that lie thy soul hath spoken!
Leave my loneliness unbroken! —quit the bust above my door!
Take thy beak from out my heart, and take thy form from off my
    door!"
                    Quoth the Raven, "Nevermore."

And the Raven, never flitting, still is sitting, still is sitting
On the pallid bust of Pallas just above my chamber door;
And his eyes have all the seeming of a demon's that is dreaming,
And the lamp-light o'er him streaming throws his shadow on
    the floor;
And my soul from out that shadow that lies floating on the floor
                Shall be lifted—nevermore!

---

pallid: pale; lacking liveliness
seeming: appearance

ANNABEL LEE
by Edgar Allan Poe

It was many and many a year ago,
    In a kingdom by the sea,
That a maiden there lived whom you may know
    By the name of Annabel Lee; —
And this maiden she lived with no other thought
    Than to love and be loved by me.

I was a child and *she* was a child,
    In this kingdom by the sea,
But we loved with a love that was more than love—
    I and my Annabel Lee—
With a love that the wingèd seraphs of Heaven
    Coveted her and me.

And this was the reason that, long ago,
    In this kingdom by the sea,
A wind blew out of a cloud, chilling
    My beautiful Annabel Lee;
So that her high-born kinsman came
    And bore her away from me,
To shut her up in a sepulchre
    In this kingdom by the sea.

---

seraphs: angels
coveted: envied
kinsman: a relative
sepulchre: a tomb

The angels, not half so happy in Heaven,
    Went envying her and me—
Yes! —that was the reason (as all men know,
    In this kingdom by the sea)
That the wind came out of the cloud by night,
    Chilling and killing my Annabel Lee.

But our love it was stronger by far than the love
    Of those who were older than we—
    Of many far wiser than we—
And neither the angels in Heaven above,
    Nor the demons down under the sea,
Can ever dissever my soul from the soul
    Of the beautiful Annabel Lee: —

For the moon never beams, without bringing me dreams
    Of the beautiful Annabel Lee,
And the stars never rise, but I feel the bright eyes
    Of the beautiful Annabel Lee; —
And so, all the night-tide, I lie down by the side
Of my darling—my darling—my life and my bride,
    In the sepulchre there by the sea—
    In her tomb by the sounding sea.

---

dissever: to separate

THE SONG OF WANDERING AENGUS

by William Butler Yeats

I went out to the hazel wood,
Because a fire was in my head,
And cut and peeled a hazel wand,
And hooked a berry to a thread;
And when white moths were on the wing,
And moth-like stars were flickering out,
I dropped the berry in a stream
And caught a little silver trout.

When I had laid it on the floor
I went to blow the fire aflame,
But something rustled on the floor,
And some one called me by my name:
It had become a glimmering girl
With apple blossom in her hair
Who called me by my name and ran
And faded through the brightening air.

Aengus: in Irish mythology, the god of love
hazel: a kind of birch tree
wand: a narrow rod

Though I am old with wandering
Through hollow lands and hilly lands,
I will find out where she has gone,
And kiss her lips and take her hands;
And walk among long dappled grass,
And pluck till time and times are done
The silver apples of the moon,
The golden apples of the sun.

dappled: spotted; marked with contrasting patches

THE WRECK OF THE HESPERUS

by Henry Wadsworth Longfellow

It was the schooner Hesperus
　　That sailed the wintry sea;
And the skipper had taken his little daughter
　　To bear him company.

Blue were her eyes as the fairy-flax,
　　Her cheeks like the dawn of day,
And her bosom white as the hawthorn buds,
　　That ope in the month of May.

The skipper he stood beside the helm,
　　His pipe was in his mouth,
And he watched how the veering flaw did blow
　　The smoke now west, now south.

Then up and spake an old sailor,
　　Had sailed to the Spanish Main,
"I pray thee, put into yonder port,
　　For I fear a hurricane.

---

schooner: a sailing ship
fairy-flax: a delicate, flowering plant
hawthorn: a plant that bears small, white, rose-like flowers
ope: open
skipper: the person in charge of a ship
helm: the wheel used to steer a ship
veering: shifting direction
flaw: a burst of wind

"Last night, the moon had a golden ring,
  And tonight no moon we see!"
The skipper he blew a whiff from his pipe,
  And a scornful laugh laughed he.

Colder and colder blew the wind,
  A gale from the Northeast,
The snow fell hissing in the brine,
  And the billows frothed like yeast.

Down came the storm, and smote amain
  The vessel in its strength;
She shuddered and paused like a frightened steed,
  Then leaped her cable's length.

"Come hither! come hither! my little daughter,
  And do not tremble so;
For I can weather the roughest gale
  That ever wind did blow."

He wrapped her warm in his seaman's coat
  Against the stinging blast;
He cut a rope from a broken spar,
  And bound her to the mast.

---

brine: salty seawater
billows: great waves
smote: struck sharply
amain: with full strength
spar: a mast; a thick, wooden pole used to support sails

"O father! I hear the church-bells ring,
    Oh say, what may it be?"
"'Tis a fog-bell on a rock-bound coast!"
    And he steered for the open sea.

"O father! I hear the sound of guns,
    Oh say, what may it be?"
"Some ship in distress, that cannot live
    In such an angry sea!"

"O father! I see a gleaming light;
    Oh say, what may it be?"
But the father answered never a word,
    A frozen corpse was he.

Lashed to the helm, all stiff and stark,
    With his face turned to the skies,
The lantern gleamed through the gleaming snow
    On his fixed and glassy eyes.

Then the maiden clasped her hands and prayed
    That savèd she might be;
And she thought of Christ, who stilled the waves
    On the Lake of Galilee.

And fast through the midnight dark and drear,
    Through the whistling sleet and snow,
Like a sheeted ghost the vessel swept
    Towards the reef of Norman's Woe.

---

lashed: bound or tied

And ever the fitful gusts between
    A sound came from the land;
It was the sound of the trampling surf
    On the rocks and the hard sea-sand.

The breakers were right beneath her bows,
    She drifted a dreary wreck,
And a whooping billow swept the crew
    Like icicles from her deck.

She struck where the white and fleecy waves
    Looked soft as carded wool,
But the cruel rocks they gored her side
    Like the horns of an angry bull.

Her rattling shrouds, all sheathed in ice,
    With the masts went by the board;
Like a vessel of glass she stove and sank,—
    Ho! ho! the breakers roared!

At daybreak, on the bleak sea-beach
    A fisherman stood aghast,
To see the form of a maiden fair
    Lashed close to a drifting mast.

---

fitful: unsteady; starting and stopping quickly and irregularly
breakers: crashing waves
gored: pierced
shrouds: ropes fixed on each side of a ship's masts
stove: crushed inward
aghast: horrified

The salt sea was frozen on her breast,
    The salt tears in her eyes;
And he saw her hair, like the brown seaweed,
    On the billows fall and rise.

Such was the wreck of the Hesperus
    In the midnight and the snow!
Christ save us all from a death like this
    On the reef of Norman's Woe!

THE CREATION

by James Weldon Johnson

And God stepped out on space,
And he looked around and said:
I'm lonely—
I'll make me a world.

And far as the eye of God could see
Darkness covered everything,
Blacker than a hundred midnights
Down in a cypress swamp.

Then God smiled,
And the light broke,
And the darkness rolled up on one side,
And the light stood shining on the other,
And God said: That's good!

Then God reached out and took the light in his hands,
And God rolled the light around in his hands
Until he made the sun;
And he set that sun a-blazing in the heavens.
And the light that was left from making the sun
God gathered it up in a shining ball
And flung it against the darkness,
Spangling the night with the moon and stars.

---

cypress: a kind of evergreen tree

Then down between
The darkness and the light
He hurled the world;
And God said: That's good!

Then God himself stepped down—
And the sun was on his right hand,
And the moon was on his left;
The stars were clustered about his head,
And the earth was under his feet.
And God walked, and where he trod
His footsteps hollowed the valleys out
And bulged the mountains up.

Then he stopped and looked and saw
That the earth was hot and barren.
So God stepped over to the edge of the world
And he spat out the seven seas—
He batted his eyes, and the lightnings flashed—
He clapped his hands, and the thunders rolled—
And the waters above the earth came down,
The cooling waters came down.

Then the green grass sprouted,
And the little red flowers blossomed,
The pine tree pointed his finger to the sky,
And the oak spread out his arms,
The lakes cuddled down in the hollows of the ground,
And the rivers ran down to the sea;

---

barren: without vegetation; not producing anything

And God smiled again,
And the rainbow appeared,
And curled itself around his shoulder.
Then God raised his arm and he waved his hand
Over the sea and over the land,
And he said: Bring forth! Bring forth!
And quicker than God could drop his hand,
Fishes and fowls
And beasts and birds
Swam the rivers and the seas,
Roamed the forests and the woods,
And split the air with their wings.
And God said: That's good!

Then God walked around,
And God looked around
On all that he had made.
He looked at his sun,
And he looked at his moon,
And he looked at his little stars;
He looked on his world
With all its living things,
And God said: I'm lonely still.

Then God sat down
On the side of a hill where he could think;
By a deep, wide river he sat down;
With his head in his hands,
God thought and thought,
Till he thought: I'll make me a man!

Up from the bed of the river
God scooped the clay;
And by the bank of the river
He kneeled him down;
And there the great God Almighty
Who lit the sun and fixed it in the sky,
Who flung the stars to the most far corner of the night,
Who rounded the earth in the middle of his hand;
This Great God,
Like a mammy bending over her baby,
Kneeled down in the dust
Toiling over a lump of clay
Till he shaped it in his own image;

Then into it he blew the breath of life,
And man became a living soul.
Amen. Amen.

SHORT STORIES

THE GLASS OF MILK

by Manuel Rojas
translated by Zoila Nelken

Propped on the starboard rail, the sailor seemed to be waiting for someone. A bundle wrapped in white paper, grease-spotted, was in his left hand; his right tended his pipe.

From behind some freight-cars, a thin youth appeared; he paused a moment, looked out to sea, and then walked on along the edge of the wharf with his hands in his pockets, idling or thinking.

When he passed in front of the ship, the sailor called out to him in English:

"I say, look here!"

The youth raised his head, and without stopping answered in the same language:

"Hello! What?"

"Are you hungry?"

There was a brief silence during which the youth seemed to be thinking, and took one shorter step as if to stop, but then replied, smiling feebly at the sailor.

"No. I'm not hungry. Thanks, sailor."

"All right."

The sailor took his pipe from his mouth, spat, and replacing it, looked away. The youth, ashamed that he had seemed to need charity, walked a little faster, as if afraid he might change his mind.

---

starboard: when looking forward, the right side of a ship
idling: doing nothing

A moment later, a gaudy tramp with a long, blond beard and blue eyes, dressed in odd rags and oversized, torn shoes, passed before the sailor, who without greeting called to him:

"Are you hungry?"

He had not yet finished the phrase when the tramp looked with shining eyes at the package the sailor held in his hand and answered hurriedly:

"Yes, sir; I'm very much hungry!"

The sailor smiled. The package flew through the air and landed in the eager hands. The hungry fellow did not even say "thanks," but sat right down on the ground, opened the still-warm bundle, and happily rubbed his hands as he saw what it contained. A port loafer might not speak English well, but he would never forgive himself if he didn't know enough to ask food from someone who did speak it.

The youth who had passed by first had stopped nearby, and had seen what happened.

He was hungry too. He had not eaten for exactly three days, three long days. And more from timidity and shame than from pride, he refused to wait by the gangways at mealtimes, hoping the generosity of the sailors would produce some package of leftovers and bits of meat. He could not do it, he would never be able to do it. And when, as just now, someone did offer him a handout, the boy refused it heroically, though he felt his hunger increase with the refusal.

---

gaudy: showy in a cheap way
port loafer: one who hangs around the docks all day doing nothing
timidity: lack of confidence; shyness; fearfulness
gangways: planks that run from a ship to the dock, on which one must
    walk to board a vessel

He had been wandering for six days around the side streets and docks of that port. An English vessel had left him there after bringing him from Punta Arenas, where he had jumped a previous ship on which he had served as captain's mess boy. He had spent a month there helping an Austrian crabber and then had stowed away on the first ship bound north.

He was discovered the day after sailing, and put to work in the boiler room. At the first large port of call, he had been put off, and there he had remained, like a bale without a label, without an acquaintance, without a penny, and without a trade.

As long as the ship was in port, the boy managed to eat, but after that… The great city that rose up beyond the back streets with their taverns and cheap inns did not attract him; it seemed a place of slavery; stale, dark, without the grand sweep of the sea; among its high walls and narrow streets people lived and died bewildered by agonizing drudgery.

The boy was gripped by that fascination of the sea which molds the most peaceful and orderly lives as a strong arm a thin rod. Although very young, he had already made several trips along the coast of South America on various ships, doing odd jobs and tasks, tasks and odd jobs which were almost useless on land.

After the ship left him, the boy walked and walked, hoping to chance upon something that would enable him to live somehow until he could get back to his home grounds; but he found nothing. The port was not very busy, and the few ships that had work would not take him on.

---

jumped…ship: without permission, left a ship on which he was employed
bale: a large, bound package
drudgery: boring and joyless tasks

The docks were swarming with confirmed tramps: sailors on the beach, like himself, who had either jumped ship or were fleeing some crime; loafers given to idleness, who kept alive one knows not how, by begging and stealing, spending their days as if they were the beads of some grimy rosary, waiting for who knows what extraordinary events, or not expecting anything; people of the strangest and most exotic races and places, and even some in whose existence one doesn't believe until one sees a living example.

The following day, convinced that he could not hold out much longer, the youth decided to resort to any means to get some food.

Walking along, he found himself in front of a ship that had docked the night before, and was loading wheat. A line of men, heavy sacks on their shoulders, shuttled from the freight-cars, across the gangplank to the hatchways of the ship's hold where the stevedores received the cargo.

He watched for a while, until he dared speak to the foreman, offering his services. He was accepted, and enthusiastically he took his place in the long line of dock workers.

During the first period of the day he worked well: but later, he began to feel tired and dizzy; he swayed as he crossed the gangplank, the heavy load on his shoulder, on seeing at his feet the opening between the side of the ship and the thick wall of the wharf, at the bottom of which the sea, stained with oil and littered with garbage, lapped quietly.

There was a brief pause at lunch time, and while some of the men went off to nearby eating places, and others ate what

---

rosary: a string of beads used, generally by Roman Catholics,
   in counting prayers
stevedores: workers who load and unload ships
lapped: slapped softly against

they had brought, the boy stretched out on the ground to rest, hiding his hunger.

He finished his day's work completely exhausted, covered with sweat, at the end of his rope. While the laborers were leaving, the boy sat on some sacks, watching for the foreman, and when the last man had gone, approached him; confused and stuttering, he asked, without explaining what was happening to him, if he could be paid immediately, or if it were possible to get an advance on his earnings.

The foreman answered that it was customary to pay at the end of the job, and that it would still be necessary to work the following day in order to finish loading the ship. One more day! On the other hand, they had never paid a cent in advance.

"But," he said, "if you need it, I could lend you about forty cents…That's all I have."

The boy thanked him for his offer with an anguished smile, and left.

Then the boy was seized by acute despair. He was hungry, hungry, hungry! Hunger doubled him over, like a heavy, broad whiplash. He saw everything through a blue haze, and he staggered like a drunk when he walked. Nevertheless, he would not have been able to complain or to shout, for his suffering was deep and exhausting; it was not pain, but anguish, the end! It seemed to him that he was flattened out by a great weight.

Suddenly he felt his entrails on fire, and he stood still. He began to bend down, down, doubling over forcibly like a rod of steel, until he thought that he would drop. At that instant, as if a window opened before him, he saw his home, the

---

anguished: greatly pained; tormented
entrails: intestines

view from it, the faces of his mother, brothers and sisters, all that he wanted and loved appeared and disappeared before his eyes shut by fatigue… Then, little by little, the giddiness passed and he began to straighten up, while the burning subsided gradually. Finally he straightened up, breathing deeply. One more hour and he would drop unconscious to the ground.

He quickened his step, as if he were fleeing another dizzy spell, and, as he walked, he made up his mind to eat anywhere, without paying, even if they shamed him, beat him, sent him to jail, anything; the main thing was to eat, eat, eat. A hundred times he mentally repeated the word: eat, eat, eat, until it lost its meaning, leaving his head feeling hot and empty.

He did not intend to run away; he would simply say to the owner, "Sir, I was hungry, hungry, hungry, and I can't pay… Do what you want."

He came to the outskirts of the city, and on one of the first streets he found a milk bar. It was a small, clean, and airy place, with little tables with marble tops. Behind the counter stood a blonde lady in a very white apron.

He chose that place. There were few passersby. He could have eaten at one of the cheap grills near the wharves but they were always full of people who gambled and drank.

There was only one customer in the milk bar. He was a little old man with glasses, who sat reading, his nose stuck between the pages of a newspaper, motionless, as if glued to his chair. On the little table there was a half-empty glass of milk.

While he waited for him to leave, the boy walked up and down the sidewalk; he felt the burning sensation in his stomach

---

subsided: lessened

returning little by little; and he waited five, ten, up to fifteen minutes. He grew tired, and stood to one side of the door, from where he cast glances like stones at the old man.

What the devil could he be reading with such attention? The boy even imagined the old man was his enemy, who knew his intentions and decided to frustrate them. He felt like entering and saying something insulting that would force the old man to leave, a rude word or phrase that would show him he had no right to sit there reading for an hour for so small a purchase.

Finally, the client finished what he was reading, or at least, interrupted it. He downed the rest of the milk in one gulp, got up slowly, paid, and walked toward the door. He went out. He was a stoop-shouldered old man, probably a carpenter or a varnisher.

Once in the street, the old man put on his glasses, stuck his nose in the newspaper again, and walked slowly away, stopping every ten steps to read more closely.

The youth waited until he was some distance away, and then entered. For a moment the boy stood by the entrance, undecided, not knowing where to sit. Finally, he chose a table and walked toward it, but halfway there he changed his mind, walked back, tripped over a chair, and finally installed himself in a corner.

The lady came, wiped the table top with a rag, and in a soft voice that had a trace of Castilian accent, asked him, "What will you have?"

"A glass of milk."

"Large?"

"Yes, large."

"Is that all?"

Castilian: related to Castile, a region of central and northern Spain

"Are there any biscuits?"

"No. Vanilla wafers."

"Well, vanilla wafers."

When the lady had turned away, he wiped his hands on his knees, rejoicing, as if he were cold and about to drink something hot.

The lady returned, and placed before him a large glass of milk, and a dish full of vanilla wafers; then she went back to her place behind the counter.

His first impulse was to drink the milk in one gulp then eat the vanilla wafers, but he immediately changed his mind. He felt the woman's eyes were watching him with curiosity and attention. He did not dare look at her; he felt that if he did she would guess his situation and his shameful intentions, and he would have to get up and leave without touching what he had ordered.

Slowly, he took a vanilla wafer and moistening it in the milk, he took a bite; he took a sip of milk and he felt the burning in his stomach diminishing, dying away. But he became aware of the reality of his desperate situation at once, and he felt something tight and hot well up inside, choking him. He realized he was about to cry, to sob aloud, and although he knew that the lady was looking at him, he could neither hold back nor undo the burning knot of tears that grew tighter and tighter. He fought it, and as he fought, he ate hurriedly, as if frightened, afraid that crying would keep him from eating. When he had finished the milk and the wafers, his eyes clouded and something hot rolled down his nose and into the glass. A terrible sob racked his whole body.

He held his head in his hands, and for a long time he cried; cried with rage, cried with shame, crying as he had never cried before.

He was hunched over crying when he felt a hand caress his tired head, and heard a woman's voice with a sweet Castilian accent say to him:

"Cry, son, cry…."

Again his eyes filled with tears and he cried as intensely as before, but this time, not with pain but with joy; he felt a great refreshing sensation spread inside him, extinguishing the hot something that had nearly strangled him. As he cried, it seemed to him that his life and feelings were cleansed like a glass under a stream of water, recovering the clearness and firmness of former days.

When the crying spell passed, he wiped his eyes and face with his handkerchief, feeling relieved. He raised his head and looked at the lady, but she was no longer looking at him, she was gazing out at the street, at a distant point in space, and her face seemed sad.

On the table before him, there was another glass of milk and another dish heaped with vanilla wafers. He ate slowly, without thinking about anything, as if nothing had happened to him, as if he were at home and his mother were that woman who was standing behind the counter.

When he finished, it had grown dark, and the place was lit by an electric light. He remained seated for a while, wondering what he would say to the lady when he left, without thinking of anything appropriate.

At last he got up and said simply, "Thank you very much, ma'am; goodbye…"

"Goodbye, son," she answered.

He went out. The wind blowing from the sea refreshed his face, still hot from weeping. He walked about aimlessly for a while, then went down a street that led to the docks. It was a very beautiful night, and large stars gleamed in the summer sky.

He thought about the blonde lady who had treated him so generously, resolving to repay her, to reward her as she deserved, when he got some money. But these thoughts of gratitude vanished with the burning of his face, until not one remained, and the recent event receded and was lost in the recesses of his past life.

Suddenly, he surprised himself humming. He straightened up happily, strode on with assurance and determination.

He came to the edge of the sea, and walked back and forth with a spring in his step; he felt like a new man, as if his inner forces, previously scattered, had reassembled and united solidly.

Then he sat down on a pile of burlap sacks; fatigue, like a tingling sensation, climbed up his legs. He looked at the sea. The lights of the wharf and ships spread over the water in a reddish-gold ripple, trembling softly. He stretched out on his back, looking up at the sky for a long time. He did not feel like thinking, or singing, or talking. He just felt alive, that was all. Then he fell asleep with his face toward the sea.

GUMPTION
by Langston Hughes

You young folks don't remember the depression, but I do. No jobs for nobody. That winter there wasn't a soul working in our house but my wife, and she was evil as she could be. She was doing a few washings now and then for the white folks—before hand laundry went out of style—so we kinder made out. But she didn't like to see me sitting around, even if I couldn't find a job. There wasn't no work to be got in our town, nor any other place, for that matter. We had a couple of roomers, a man and his girl friend; but they were out of a job also. And, like me and my wife, they hadn't been in town long enough to get any consideration, since the relief folks were hard on strangers. All of us was just managing to get by on beans and mush all winter.

One cold February morning we was sitting around the stove in the kitchen trying to keep warm, the roomers and me, my wife was ironing, when who should pass by outside in the alley but old man Oyster and his son.

"There goes Oyster and that boy of his," I said, "ragged as a jay-bird, both of 'em."

"They ain't even on relief work, is they?" Jack, the roomer, asked.

"They did have a few hours' work a month," I answered. "They messed up, though."

"Messed up, you call it, heh?" my wife put in, in her nervous way. "Well, they got gumption, anyhow. They told

---

relief: public program to assist needy people
gumption: spunk; boldness; initiative

them white folks up yonder in the office just what they thought of 'em. That's what they did."

"And look at 'em now," I said, "going through the alley looking for something to eat."

"Well, they got gumption," my wife yelled, "and that's something."

"You can't eat gumption," Jack remarked, which made my wife mad.

"You can't eat sitting-around-on-your-rumpus, neither," she broke out, slamming her iron down on the white man's shirt and looking real hard at our roomer—a look that said, You oughtn't to talk, cause you ain't paid your rent for a month.

I sure was glad I hadn't said nothing, boy.

"What's it all about?" Jack's girl asked. "What's old man Oyster done to get in bad with them relief folks, Miss Clara?"

She had heard about it before from me, but she just wanted to get my wife to running her mouth—and keep her mind off the fact that they hadn't paid their rent that month.

"You ain't heard?" my wife said, choosing a new hot iron. "It's a story worth telling, to my mind, cause they got *gumption*—them Oysters." She looked hard at Jack and me. "Now, old man Oyster—this story goes way back, child—he ain't never amounted to much, just poor and honest. But he always did want to make something out of that boy o' his'n, Charlie—little and runty as he was. He worked hard to do it, too. He portered, bellhopped, did road work, did anything he could get to do. Kept that boy in school after his wife died,

---

portered: carried bags at a train or bus station
bellhopped: carried bags at a hotel

washed his ears, kept him clean, tried to make a gentleman out of him—and that boy did pretty well. Grew up and took a commercial bookkeeping-typewriter course in the school, and come out Grade A. *Grade A*, I'm telling you. Graduated and got a job with the white folks. Yes, sir! First time I ever heard tell of a colored boy typewriting or keeping books or anything like that in this white man's town. But Mr. Bartelson what owned the coalyard and fuel office where young Oyster worked, he was from Maine and didn't have no prejudice to speak of, so he gave this colored boy a chance in his place. And was them white truck drivers jealous—seeing a Negro working in the office and they out driving trucks! But old man Oyster's boy was *prepared*. I'm telling you, *prepared!* He had a good education and could do the work, black as he was. And he was lucky to find somebody to give him a break, because you know and I know you don't see no colored men working in white folks' offices nowhere hardly.

"Well, sir, old man Oyster was proud as he could be of his boy. We was all proud. The church was proud. The white business school what graduated him was proud. Everything went fine for two or three years. Oyster and Charlie even started to buy a little house, cause the old man was working on the road digging for forty cents an hour. Then the depression came. They stopped building roads, and folks stopped buying fuel to keep warm by. Poor old man Bartelson what owned the coalyard finally had to close up, bankrupted and broke—which left young Oyster without a job, like the rest of us. Old man Oyster was jobless, too, cause the less roads they built and sewers they laid, the less work they gave to colored folks, and give it to the white instead. You know how it is—first to be fired and last to be hired."

Clara was just a-ironing and a-talking. "Then along come

this Government relief and WPA and everybody thought times was surely gonna get better. Well, they ain't got no better, leastwise not for colored. Everybody in this town's on relief now but me and you-all—what ain't been here long enough to be in it. I've still got a few washings to do and a little house cleaning now and then, thank God! But look at Sylvester," pointing at me. "They have done cut every porter off at the bus station but one. And Syl is jobless as a greyhound.

"Anyhow, to go ahead with Oyster, it were a crying shame to see this poor old man and that fine young colored boy out of work—and they both ambitious, and steady, and good race men. Well, when relief opened up and they started giving out so many hours of work a month, they put old man Oyster back on the road. Now, his boy, Charlie, ain't never done no kind of work like road work, being a office man. But he thought he'd have to do it, too, and Charlie wasn't objecting, mind you—when the Government opened up a office for what they calls white-collar workers. All the white folks what's been doing office work in good times, insurance people and store clerks and such, they went there to get the kind o' work they was used to doing. Oyster's son went, too. But don't you know they discriminated against him! Yes, sir—the Government discriminating him because he were black! They said, 'You're not no office worker,' in spite of all the proofs Charlie had that he were in Mr. Bartelson's office for three years—the letter Bartelson gave him and all. But they sent old man Oyster's boy right on out yonder to work on the road with his father.

"Well, that made the old man mad. He said, 'What am I working all these years for you, educating you to come out here and dig on the road with me, and you with a education?'

WPA: Works Progress Administration, a government program created during the Depression to help provide jobs

"The old man stopped his work then and there that morning, laid off, and went right on up to that government office to see the white man about it. And that's where the trouble commenced!"

Clara was just a-talking and a-ironing. "The Government white man said, 'You ought to be glad for your boy to get any kind o' work, these days and times. You can't be picking and choosing now.'

"But old man Oyster stood there and argued with the man for his son's rights. That's why I say he's got *gumption*. He said, 'I ain't asking to be picking and choosing, and I ain't asked nothing for *myself*. I'm speaking about that boy o' mine. Charlie's got a education. True, he's colored, but he's worked for three years in a office for one of the finest white men that ever lived and breathed, Mr. Bartelson. Charlie's got experience. My boy's a typewriter and a bookkeeper. What for you send him out to work on a road with me? Ain't this the place what's giving all the white folks jobs doing what they used to doing and know how to do? My boy ain't know nothing about no pick and shovel. Why don't you treat Charlie Oyster like you do the rest of the people and give him some o' his kind o' work?'

"'We have no office jobs here for Negroes,' said the man, right flat out like that. 'That's why I sent your son over where they give out road work. I classify all Negroes as laborers on our relief rolls.'

"Well, that made old man Oyster mad as hell. He said, 'Drat it, I'm a citizen! Is that what WPA is for—to bring more discrimination than what is? I want to know why my boy can't be a typewriter like the rest of 'em what's got training, even if it is on relief. If he could work in a white man's office, ain't he good enough to get work from you—and you the gobernment?'

"Well, this made the white man mad, and he yelled, 'You must be one o' them Communists, ain't you?' And he pressed some kind o' buzzer and sent out for a cop.

"Now, old man Oyster ain't never had no trouble of any kind in this town before, but when them cops started to put their hands on him and throw him out o' that office, he raised sand. He was right, too! But them cops didn't see it that way, and one of 'em brought his stock down on that old man's head and knocked him out.

"When Oyster come to, he was in jail.

"Then old man Oyster's son showed he was a man! Charlie heard about the trouble when he come home from off the road that evening, and he went to the jail to see his papa, boiling mad. When he heard how it was, that white man calling the cops in to beat up his father, he said, 'Pa, I'll be in jail here with you tomorrow.' And sure enough, he was. He went up to that there white-collar relief office the next morning and beat that white man so bad, he ain't got over it yet.

"'The idea,' young Oyster said, 'of you having my father knocked down and dragged out because he came here to talk to you like a citizen about our rights! Who are you anyway, any more'n me? Try to throw me out o' here and I'll beat you to a pulp first!'

"Well, that man reached for the buzzer again to call some more cops. When he reached, young Oyster had him! It would a-done me good to see the way that black boy give that white man a fit—cause he turned him every way but loose. When the cops come, they put Charlie in jail all right— but that white man was beat by then! The idea of relief coming here adding prejudice to what we already got, and times as hard as they is."

Clara planked down her iron on the stove. "Anyhow, they didn't keep them Oysters in jail very long, neither father or son. Old Judge Murray give 'em a month apiece, suspended sentence, and let 'em out. But when they got out o' jail, don't you know them relief people wouldn't give Oyster and his boy no more work a-tall! No, sir! They told 'em they wasn't feeding no black reds. Now old man Oyster nor Charlie neither ain't never heard o' Communists—but that's what they called 'em just cause they went up there and fought for what they ought to have. They didn't win—they're out there in the alleys now hauling trash. But they got gumption!"

"You can't live on gumption," I said, trying to be practical.

"No, but you can choke on shame!" my wife yelled, looking hard at Jack and me. "I ain't never seen you-all fighting for nothing yet. Lord knows you both bad enough off to go out and raise hell somewhere and get something!" She put the iron down with a bang. "If I had a young boy, I'd want him to be like Oyster's son, and not take after none of you —sitting around behind the stove talking 'bout you 'can't live on gump-tion.' You can't live on it cause you ain't got none, that's why! Get up from behind that stove, get out o' here, both of you, and bring me something back I can use—bread, money, or a job, I don't care which. Get up and go on! Scat!"

She waved her iron in the air and looked like she meant to bring it down on my head instead of on a shirt. So Jack and me had to leave that nice warm house and go out in the cold and scuffle. There was no peace at home that morning, I mean. I had to try and work up a little gumption.

---

reds: slang term for "communists"

TO BUILD A FIRE
by Jack London

Day had broken cold and grey, exceedingly cold and grey, when the man turned aside from the main Yukon trail and climbed the high earth-bank, where a dim and little-traveled trail led eastward through the fat spruce timberland. It was a steep bank, and he paused for breath at the top, excusing the act to himself by looking at his watch. It was nine o'clock. There was no sun nor hint of sun, though there was not a cloud in the sky. It was a clear day, and yet there seemed an intangible pall over the face of things, a subtle gloom that made the day dark, and that was due to the absence of sun. This fact did not worry the man. He was used to the lack of sun. It had been days since he had seen the sun, and he knew that a few more days must pass before that cheerful orb, due south, would just peep above the sky line and dip immediately from view.

The man flung a look back along the way he had come. The Yukon lay a mile wide and hidden under three feet of ice. On top of this ice were as many feet of snow. It was all pure white, rolling in gentle undulations where the ice jams of the freeze-up had formed. North and south, as far as his eye could see, it was unbroken white, save for a dark hairline

---

Yukon: a territory in northwestern Canada; also, a river that runs through
 the region
intangible: incapable of being touched
pall: something that covers and produces a gloomy effect; a heavy cloth
 thrown over a coffin
undulations: wave-like appearances; wavy, curving forms

that curved and twisted from around the spruce-covered island to the south, and that curved and twisted away into the north, where it disappeared behind another spruce-covered island. This dark hairline was the trail—the main trail—that led south five hundred miles to the Chilcoot Pass, Dyea, and salt water; and that led north seventy miles to Dawson, and still on to the north a thousand miles to Nulato, and finally to St. Michael on Bering Sea, a thousand miles and half a thousand more.

But all this—the mysterious, far-reaching hairline trail, the absence of sun from the sky, the tremendous cold, and the strangeness and weirdness of it all—made no impression on the man. It was not because he was long used to it. He was a newcomer in the land, a *chechaquo*, and this was his first winter. The trouble with him was that he was without imagination. He was quick and alert in the things of life, but only in the things, and not in the significances. Fifty degrees below zero meant eighty-odd degrees of frost. Such fact impressed him as being cold and uncomfortable, and that was all. It did not lead him to meditate upon his frailty as a creature of temperature, and upon man's frailty in general, able only to live within certain narrow limits of heat and cold; and from there on it did not lead him to the conjectural

---

Chilcoot Pass (also spelled *Chilkoot*): a pass in the mountains on the border between British Columbia and Alaska
Dyea: at one time, a town south of the Chilcoot Pass
Dawson: a town on the Yukon River in the western Yukon Territory
Nulato: a town in Alaska
St. Michael: a port in Alaska
Bering Sea: a body of water that extends from the Pacific Ocean northward between Siberia and Alaska
chechaquo: a newcomer; a tenderfoot
meditate: to think about; to reflect on
conjectural: based on guesswork; concluded without evidence or proof

field of immortality and man's place in the universe. Fifty degrees below zero stood for a bite of frost that hurt and that must be guarded against by the use of mittens, ear-flaps, warm moccasins, and thick socks. Fifty degrees below zero was to him just precisely fifty degrees below zero. That there should be anything more to it than that was a thought that never entered his head.

As he turned to go on, he spat speculatively. There was a sharp, explosive crackle that startled him. He spat again. And again, in the air, before it could fall to the snow, the spittle crackled. He knew that at fifty below spittle crackled on the snow, but this spittle had crackled in the air. Undoubtedly it was colder than fifty below—how much colder he did not know. But the temperature did not matter. He was bound for the old claim on the left fork of Henderson Creek, where the boys were already. They had come over across the divide from the Indian Creek country, while he had come the roundabout way to take a look at the possibilities of getting out logs in the spring from the islands in the Yukon. He would be in to camp by six o'clock; a bit after dark, it was true, but the boys would be there, a fire would be going, and a hot supper would be ready. As for lunch, he pressed his hand against the protruding bundle under his jacket. It was also under his shirt, wrapped up in a handkerchief and lying against the naked skin. It was the only way to keep the biscuits from freezing. He smiled agreeably to himself as he thought of those biscuits, each cut open and sopped in bacon grease, and each enclosing a generous slice of fried bacon.

_____

speculatively: in a manner intended to test an idea or theory
protruding: jutting out; pushing forward

He plunged in among the big spruce trees. The trail was faint. A foot of snow had fallen since the last sled had passed over, and he was glad he was without a sled, traveling light. In fact, he carried nothing but the lunch wrapped in the handkerchief. He was surprised, however, at the cold. It certainly was cold, he concluded, as he rubbed his numbed nose and cheekbones with his mittened hand. He was a warm-whiskered man, but the hair on his face did not protect the high cheekbones and the eager nose that thrust itself aggressively into the frosty air.

At the man's heels trotted a dog, a big native husky, the proper wolf dog, grey-coated and without any visible or temperamental difference from its brother, the wild wolf. The animal was depressed by the tremendous cold. It knew that it was no time for traveling. Its instinct told it a truer tale than was told to the man by the man's judgment. In reality, it was not merely colder than fifty below zero; it was colder than sixty below, than seventy below. It was seventy-five below zero. Since the freezing point is thirty-two above zero, it meant that one hundred and seven degrees of frost obtained. The dog did not know anything about thermometers. Possibly in its brain there was no sharp consciousness of a condition of very cold such as was in the man's brain. But the brute had its instinct. It experienced a vague but menacing apprehension that subdued it and made it slink along at the man's heels, and that made it question eagerly every unwonted movement of the man as if expecting him to go into camp or to seek

---

temperamental: relating to one's disposition, one's way of thinking
   and behaving
menacing: threatening
apprehension: suspicion of fear; foreboding
unwonted: not usual; out of the ordinary

shelter somewhere and build a fire. The dog had learned fire, and it wanted fire, or else to burrow under the snow and cuddle its warmth away from the air.

The frozen moisture of its breathing had settled on its fur in a fine powder of frost, and especially were its jowls, muzzle, and eyelashes whitened by its crystalled breath. The man's red beard and moustache were likewise frosted, but more solidly, the deposit taking the form of ice and increasing with every warm, moist breath he exhaled. Also, the man was chewing tobacco, and the muzzle of ice held his lips so rigidly that he was unable to clear his chin when he expelled the juice. The result was that a crystal beard of the color and solidity of amber was increasing its length on his chin. If he fell down it would shatter itself, like glass, into brittle fragments. But he did not mind the appendage. It was the penalty all tobacco chewers paid in that country, and he had been out before in two cold snaps. They had not been so cold as this, he knew, but by the spirit thermometer at Sixty Mile he knew they had been registered at fifty below and at fifty-five.

He held on through the level stretch of woods for several miles, crossed a wide flat, and dropped down a bank to the frozen bed of a small stream. This was Henderson Creek, and he knew he was ten miles from the forks. He looked at his watch. It was ten o'clock. He was making four miles an hour, and he calculated that he would arrive at the forks at half-past twelve. He decided to celebrate that event by eating his lunch there.

The dog dropped in again at his heels, with a tail drooping discouragement, as the man swung along the creek

---

appendage: something attached to a larger thing, such as a limb of a body

bed. The furrow of the old sled trail was plainly visible, but a dozen inches of snow covered the marks of the last runners. In a month no man had come up or down that silent creek. The man held steadily on. He was not much given to thinking, and just then particularly he had nothing to think about save that he would eat lunch at the forks and that at six o'clock he would be in camp with the boys. There was nobody to talk to and, had there been, speech would have been impossible because of the ice muzzle on his mouth. So he continued monotonously to chew tobacco and to increase the length of his amber beard.

Once in a while the thought reiterated itself that it was very cold and that he had never experienced such cold. As he walked along he rubbed his cheekbones and nose with the back of his mittened hand. He did this automatically, now and again changing hands. But rub as he would, the instant he stopped his cheekbones went numb, and the following instant the end of his nose went numb. He was sure to frost his cheeks; he knew that, and experienced a pang of regret that he had not devised a nose strap of the sort Bud wore in cold snaps. Such a strap passed across the cheeks, as well, and saved them. But it didn't matter much, after all. What were frosted cheeks? A bit painful, that was all; they were never serious.

Empty as the man's mind was of thoughts, he was keenly observant, and he noticed the changes in the creek, the curves and bends and timber jams, and always he sharply noted where he placed his feet. Once, coming around a bend, he shied abruptly, like a startled horse, curved away from the

---

monotonously: in a tiresome and unvarying way
reiterated: repeated

place where he had been walking, and retreated several paces back along the trail. The creek he knew was frozen clear to the bottom—no creek could contain water in that arctic winter—but he knew also that there were springs that bubbled out from the hillsides and ran along under the snow and on top of the ice of the creek. He knew that the coldest snaps never froze these springs, and he knew likewise their danger. They were traps. They hid pools of water under the snow that might be three inches deep, or three feet. Sometimes a skin of ice half an inch thick covered them, and in turn was covered by the snow. Sometimes there were alternate layers of water and ice-skin, so that when one broke through he kept on breaking through for a while, sometimes wetting himself to the waist.

That was why he had shied in such panic. He had felt the give under his feet and heard the crackle of a snow-hidden ice-skin. And to get his feet wet in such a temperature meant trouble and danger. At the very least it meant delay, for he would be forced to stop and build a fire, and under its protection to bare his feet while he dried his socks and moccasins. He stood and studied the creek bed and its banks, and decided that the flow of water came from the right. He reflected awhile, rubbing his nose and cheeks, then skirted to the left, stepping gingerly and testing the footing for each step. Once clear of the danger, he took a fresh chew of tobacco and swung along at his four-mile gait.

In the course of the next two hours he came upon several similar traps. Usually the snow above the hidden pools had a sunken, candied appearance that advertised the danger. Once again, however, he had a close call; and once, suspecting

---

gingerly: cautiously; very carefully

danger, he compelled the dog to go on in front. The dog did not want to go. It hung back until the man shoved it forward, and then it went quickly across the white, unbroken surface. Suddenly it broke through, floundered to one side, and got away to firmer footing. It had wet its forefeet and legs, and almost immediately the water that clung to it turned to ice.

It made quick efforts to lick the ice off its legs, then dropped down in the snow and began to bite out the ice that had formed between the toes. This was a matter of instinct. To permit the ice to remain would mean sore feet. It did not know this. It merely obeyed the mysterious prompting that arose from the deep crypts of its being. But the man knew, having achieved a judgment on the subject, and he removed the mitten from his right hand and helped tear out the ice particles. He did not expose his fingers more than a minute, and was astonished at the swift numbness that smote them. It certainly was cold. He pulled on the mitten hastily, and beat the hand savagely across his chest.

At twelve o'clock the day was at its brightest. Yet the sun was too far south on its winter journey to clear the horizon. The bulge of the earth intervened between it and Henderson Creek, where the man walked under a clear sky at noon and cast no shadow. At half-past twelve, to the minute, he arrived at the forks of the creek. He was pleased at the speed he had made. If he kept it up, he would certainly be with the boys by six. He unbuttoned his jacket and shirt and drew forth his lunch. The action consumed no more than a quarter of a minute, yet in that brief moment the numbness laid hold of the exposed fingers. He did not put the mitten on, but,

---

compelled: forced; urged
smote: struck suddenly

instead, struck the fingers a dozen sharp smashes against his leg. Then he sat down on a snow-covered log to eat. The sting that followed upon the striking of his fingers against his leg ceased so quickly that he was startled, he had had no chance to take a bite of biscuit. He struck the fingers repeatedly and returned them to the mitten, baring the other hand for the purpose of eating. He tried to take a mouthful, but the ice-muzzle prevented. He had forgotten to build a fire and thaw out. He chuckled at his foolishness, and as he chuckled he noted the numbness creeping into the exposed fingers. Also, he noted that the stinging which had first come to his toes when he sat down was already passing away. He wondered whether the toes were warm or numbed. He moved them inside the moccasins and decided that they were numbed.

He pulled the mitten on hurriedly and stood up. He was a bit frightened. He stamped up and down until the stinging returned into the feet. It certainly was cold, was his thought. That man from Sulphur Creek had spoken the truth when telling how cold it sometimes got in the country. And he had laughed at him at the time! That showed one must not be too sure of things. There was no mistake about it, it was cold. He strode up and down, stamping his feet and threshing his arms, until reassured by the returning warmth. Then he got out matches and proceeded to make a fire. From the undergrowth, where high water of the previous spring had lodged a supply of seasoned twigs, he got his firewood. Working carefully from a small beginning, he soon had a roaring fire, over which he thawed the ice from his face and in the protection of which he ate his biscuits. For the moment the cold of space was outwitted. The dog took satisfaction in the fire, stretching out close enough for warmth and far enough away to escape being singed.

When the man had finished, he filled his pipe and took his comfortable time over a smoke. Then he pulled on his mittens, settled the ear flaps of his cap firmly about his ears, and took the creek trail up the left fork. The dog was disappointed and yearned back toward the fire. This man did not know cold. Possibly all the generations of his ancestry had been ignorant of cold, of real cold, of cold one hundred and seven degrees below freezing point. But the dog knew; all its ancestry knew, and it had inherited the knowledge. And it knew that it was not good to walk abroad in such fearful cold. It was the time to lie snug in a hole in the snow and wait for a curtain of cloud to be drawn across the face of outer space whence this cold came. On the other hand, there was no keen intimacy between the dog and the man. The one was the toil slave of the other, and the only caresses it had ever received were the caresses of the whip lash and of harsh and menacing throat sounds that threatened the whip lash. So the dog made no effort to communicate its apprehension to the man. It was not concerned in the welfare of the man; it was for its own sake that it yearned back toward the fire. But the man whistled, and spoke to it with the sound of whip lashes, and the dog swung in at the man's heels and followed after.

The man took a chew of tobacco and proceeded to start a new amber beard. Also, his moist breath quickly powdered with white his moustache, eyebrows, and lashes. There did not seem to be so many springs on the left fork of the Henderson, and for half an hour the man saw no signs of any. And then it happened. At a place where there were no signs, where the soft, unbroken snow seemed to advertise solidity beneath, the man broke through. It was not deep.

---

intimacy: close familiarity

He wetted himself half-way to the knees before he floundered out to the firm crust.

He was angry, and cursed his luck aloud. He had hoped to get into camp with the boys at six o'clock, and this would delay him an hour, for he would have to build a fire and dry out his footgear. This was imperative at that low temperature—he knew that much; and he turned aside to the bank, which he climbed. On top, tangled in the underbrush about the trunks of several small spruce trees, was a high-water deposit of dry firewood—sticks and twigs principally, but also larger portions of seasoned branches and fine, dry, last-year's grasses. He threw down several large pieces on top of the snow. This served for a foundation and prevented the young flame from drowning itself in the snow it otherwise would melt. The flame he got by touching a match to a small shred of birch bark that he took from his pocket. This burned even more readily than paper. Placing it on the foundation, he fed the young flame with wisps of dry grass and with the tiniest dry twigs.

He worked slowly and carefully, keenly aware of his danger. Gradually, as the flame grew stronger, he increased the size of the twigs with which he fed it. He squatted in the snow, pulling the twigs out from their entanglement in the brush and feeding directly to the flame. He knew there must be no failure. When it is seventy-five below zero, a man must not fail in his first attempt to build a fire—that is, if his feet are wet. If his feet are dry, and he fails, he can run along the trail for half a mile and restore his circulation. But the circulation of wet and freezing feet cannot be restored by running when it is seventy-five below. No matter how fast he runs, the wet feet will freeze the harder.

---

imperative: necessary

All this the man knew. The old-timer on Sulphur Creek had told him about it the previous fall, and now he was appreciating the advice. Already all sensation had gone out of his feet. To build the fire he had been forced to remove his mittens, and the fingers had quickly gone numb. His pace of four miles an hour had kept his heart pumping blood to the surface of his body and to all the extremities. But the instant he stopped, the action of the pump eased down. The cold of space smote the unprotected tip of the planet, and he, being on that unprotected tip, received the full force of the blow. The blood of his body recoiled before it. The blood was alive, like the dog, and like the dog it wanted to hide away and cover itself up from the fearful cold. So long as he walked four miles an hour, he pumped that blood, willy-nilly, to the surface; but now it ebbed away and sank down into the recesses of his body. The extremities were the first to feel its absence. His wet feet froze the faster, and his exposed fingers numbed the faster, though they had not yet begun to freeze. Nose and cheeks were already freezing, while the skin of all his body chilled as it lost its blood.

But he was safe. Toes and nose and cheeks would be only touched by the frost, for the fire was beginning to burn with strength. He was feeding it with twigs the size of his finger. In another minute he would be able to feed it with branches the size of his wrist, and then he could remove his wet footgear, and, while it dried, he could keep his naked feet warm by the fire, rubbing them at first, of course, with snow. The fire was a success. He was safe. He remembered the advice of the old-timer on Sulphur Creek, and smiled. The old-timer had been very serious in laying down the law that

---

extremities: limbs of the body

no man must travel alone in the Klondike after fifty below. Well, here he was; he had had the accident; he was alone; and he had saved himself. Those old-timers were rather womanish, some of them, he thought. All a man had to do was to keep his head, and he was all right. Any man who was a man could travel alone. But it was surprising, the rapidity with which his cheeks and nose were freezing. And he had not thought his fingers could go lifeless in so short a time. Lifeless they were, for he could scarcely make them move together to grip a twig, and they seemed remote from his body and from him. When he touched a twig, he had to look and see whether or not he had hold of it. The wires were pretty well down between him and his finger-ends.

All of which counted for little. There was the fire, snapping and crackling and promising life with every dancing flame. He started to untie his moccasins. They were coated with ice; the thick German socks were like sheaths of iron halfway to the knees; and the moccasin strings were like rods of steel all twisted and knotted as by some conflagration. For a moment he tugged with his numbed fingers, then, realizing the folly of it, he drew his sheath knife.

But before he could cut the strings, it happened. It was his own fault or, rather, his mistake. He should not have built the fire under the spruce tree. He should have built it in the open. But it had been easier to pull the twigs from the brush and drop them directly on the fire. Now the tree under which he had done this carried a weight of snow on its boughs. No wind had blown for weeks, and each bough was fully freighted.

Klondike: a region of the Yukon Territory in northwest Canada, on the
   Alaska border
conflagration: a raging, destructive fire

Each time he had pulled a twig he had communicated a slight agitation to the tree—an imperceptible agitation, so far as he was concerned, but an agitation sufficient to bring about the disaster. High up in the tree one bough capsized its load of snow. This fell on the boughs beneath, capsizing them. This process continued, spreading out and involving the whole tree. It grew like an avalanche, and it descended without warning upon the man and the fire, and the fire was blotted out! Where it had burned was a mantle of fresh and disordered snow.

The man was shocked. It was as though he had just heard his own sentence of death. For a moment he sat and stared at the spot where the fire had been. Then he grew very calm. Perhaps the old-timer on Sulphur Creek was right. If he had only had a trail-mate he would have been in no danger now. The trail-mate could have built the fire. Well, it was up to him to build the fire over again, and this second time there must be no failure. Even if he succeeded, he would most likely lose some toes. His feet must be badly frozen by now, and there would be some time before the second fire was ready.

Such were his thoughts, but he did not sit and think them. He was busy all the time they were passing through his mind. He made a new foundation for a fire, this time in the open, where no treacherous tree could blot it out. Next, he gathered dry grasses and tiny twigs from the high-water flotsam. He could not bring his fingers together to pull them out, but he was able to gather them by the handful. In this

----

agitation: motion
imperceptible: not noticeable
capsized: caused to tip over; overturned
flotsam: floating debris (or in this case, the material left behind by waters
   that have receded)

way he got many rotten twigs and bits of green moss that were undesirable, but it was the best he could do. He worked methodically, even collecting an armful of the larger branches to be used later when the fire gathered strength. And all the while the dog sat and watched him, a certain yearning wistfulness in its eyes, for it looked upon him as the fire provider, and the fire was slow in coming.

When all was ready, the man reached in his pocket for a second piece of birch bark. He knew the bark was there, and, though he could not feel it with his fingers, he could hear its crisp rustling as he fumbled for it. Try as he would, he could not clutch hold of it. And all the time, in his consciousness, was the knowledge that each instant his feet were freezing. This thought tended to put him in a panic, but he fought against it and kept calm. He pulled on his mittens with his teeth, and threshed his arms back and forth, beating his hands with all his might against his sides. He did this sitting down, and he stood up to do it; and all the while the dog sat in the snow, its wolf brush of a tail curled around warmly over its forefeet, its sharp wolf ears pricked forward intently as it watched the man. And the man as he beat and threshed with his arms and hands, felt a great surge of envy as he regarded the creature that was warm and secure in its natural covering.

After a time he was aware of the first far-away signals of sensation in his beaten fingers. The faint tingling grew stronger till it evolved into a stinging ache that was excruciating, but which the man hailed with satisfaction. He stripped the mitten from his right hand and fetched forth the birch bark. The exposed fingers were quickly going numb again. Next

---

excruciating: extremely painful

he brought out his bunch of sulphur matches. But the tremendous cold had already driven the life out of his fingers. In his effort to separate one match from the others, the whole bunch fell in the snow. He tried to pick it out of the snow, but failed. The dead fingers could neither touch nor clutch. He was very careful. He drove the thought of his freezing feet, and nose, and cheeks, out of his mind, devoting his whole soul to the matches. He watched, using the sense of vision in place of that of touch, and when he saw his fingers on each side of the bunch, he closed them—that is, he willed to close them, for the wires were drawn, and the fingers did not obey. He pulled the mitten on the right hand, and beat it fiercely against his knee. Then, with both mittened hands, he scooped the bunch of matches, along with much snow, into his lap. Yet he was no better off.

After some manipulation he managed to get the bunch between the heels of his mittened hands. In this fashion he carried it to his mouth. The ice crackled and snapped when by a violent effort he opened his mouth. He drew the lower jaw in, curled the upper lip out of the way, and scraped the bunch with his upper teeth in order to separate a match. He succeeded in getting one, which he dropped on his lap. He was no better off. He could not pick it up. Then he devised a way. He picked it up in his teeth and scratched it on his leg. Twenty times he scratched before he succeeded in lighting it. As it flamed he held it with his teeth to the birch bark. But the burning brimstone went up his nostrils and into his lungs, causing him to cough spasmodically. The match fell into the snow and went out.

---

brimstone: sulfur (used in matches)
spasmodically: fitfully; in sharp jerks

The old-timer on Sulphur Creek was right, he thought in the moment of controlled despair that ensued: after fifty below, a man should travel with a partner. He beat his hands, but failed in exciting any sensation. Suddenly he bared both hands, removing the mittens with his teeth. He caught the whole bunch between the heels of his hands. His arm muscles not being frozen enabled him to press the hand heels tightly against the matches. Then he scratched the bunch along his leg. It flared into flame, seventy sulphur matches at once! There was no wind to blow them out. He kept his head to one side to escape the strangling fumes, and held the blazing bunch to the birch bark. As he so held it, he became aware of sensation in his hand. His flesh was burning. He could smell it. Deep down below the surface he could feel it. The sensation developed into pain that grew acute. And still he endured it, holding the flame of the matches clumsily to the bark that would not light readily because his own burning hands were in the way, absorbing most of the flame.

At last, when he could endure no more, he jerked his hands apart. The blazing matches fell sizzling into the snow, but the birch bark was alight. He began laying dry grasses and the tiniest twigs on the flame. He could not pick and choose, for he had to lift the fuel between the heels of his hands. Small pieces of rotten wood and green moss clung to the twigs, and he bit them off as well as he could with his teeth. He cherished the flame carefully and awkwardly. It meant life, and it must not perish. The withdrawal of blood from the surface of his body now made him begin to shiver, and he grew more awkward. A large piece of green moss fell squarely on the little fire. He tried to poke it out with his fingers, but his shivering frame made him poke too far, and he disrupted the nucleus of the little fire, the burning grasses and tiny twigs separating and scattering. He tried to poke them together again, but in spite of the tenseness of the effort, his shivering got away with him, and the twigs were hopelessly scattered. Each twig gushed a puff of smoke and went out. The fire provider had failed. As he looked apathetically about him, his eyes chanced on the dog, sitting across the ruins of the fire from him, in the snow, making restless, hunching movements, slightly lifting one forefoot and then the other, shifting its weight back and forth on them with wistful eagerness.

The sight of the dog put a wild idea into his head. He remembered the tale of the man, caught in a blizzard, who killed a steer and crawled inside the carcass, and so was saved. He would kill the dog and bury his hands in the warm body until the numbness went out of them. Then he could build another fire. He spoke to the dog, calling it to him; but in his voice was a strange note of fear that frightened the animal, who had never known the man to speak in such way before. Something was the matter, and its suspicious nature sensed danger—it knew not what danger but somewhere, somehow, in its brain arose an apprehension of the man. It flattened its ears down at the sound of the man's voice, and its restless, hunching movements and the liftings and shiftings of its forefeet became more pronounced; but it would not come to the man. He got on his hands and knees and crawled toward the dog. This unusual posture again excited suspicion, and the animal sidled mincingly away.

---

nucleus: central part; core
apathetically: indifferently; in a way showing little interest or concern
sidled: edged away

The man sat up in the snow for a moment and struggled for calmness. Then he pulled on his mittens, by means of his teeth, and got upon his feet. He glanced down at first in order to assure himself that he was really standing up, for the absence of sensation in his feet left him unrelated to the earth. His erect position in itself started to drive the webs of suspicion from the dog's mind; and when he spoke peremptorily, with the sound of whip lashes in his voice, the dog rendered its customary allegiance and came to him. As it came within reaching distance, the man lost his control. His arms flashed out to the dog, and he experienced genuine surprise when he discovered that his hands could not clutch, that there was neither bend nor feeling in the fingers. He had forgotten for the moment that they were frozen and that they were freezing more and more. All this happened quickly, and before the animal could get away, he encircled its body with his arms. He sat down in the snow, and in this fashion held the dog, while it snarled and whined and struggled.

But it was all he could do, hold its body encircled in his arms and sit there. He realized that he could not kill the dog. There was no way to do it. With his helpless hands he could neither draw nor hold his sheath knife nor throttle the animal. He released it, and it plunged wildly away, with tail between its legs, and still snarling. It halted forty feet away and surveyed him curiously, with ears sharply pricked forward. The man looked down at his hands in order to locate them, and found them hanging on the ends of his arms. It struck him as curious that one should have to use his eyes in order to find out where his hands were. He began threshing his arms back and forth, beating the mittened hands against his

peremptorily: in a curt and commanding manner

sides. He did this for five minutes, violently, and his heart pumped enough blood up to the surface to put a stop to his shivering. But no sensation was aroused in the hands. He had an impression that they hung like weights on the ends of his arms, but when he tried to run the impression down, he could not find it.

A certain fear of death, dull and oppressive, came to him. This fear quickly became poignant as he realized that it was no longer a mere matter of freezing his fingers and toes, or of losing his hands and feet, but that it was a matter of life and death with the chances against him. This threw him into a panic, and he turned and ran up the creek bed along the old, dim trail. The dog joined in behind and kept up with him. He ran blindly, without intention, in fear such as he had never known in his life. Slowly, as he plowed and floundered through the snow, he began to see things again—the banks of the creek, the old timber jams, the leafless aspens, and the sky. The running made him feel better. He did not shiver. Maybe, if he ran on, his feet would thaw out; and, anyway, if he ran far enough, he would reach camp and the boys. Without doubt he would lose some fingers and toes and some of his face; but the boys would take care of him, and save the rest of him when he got there. And at the same time there was another thought in his mind that said he would never get to the camp and the boys; that it was too many miles away, that the freezing had too great a start on him, and that he would soon be stiff and dead. This thought he kept in the background and refused to consider. Sometimes it pushed itself forward

---

oppressive: depressing; heavily weighing on the spirit
poignant: deeply emotional; affecting the emotions in a sharp, painful way

and demanded to be heard, but he thrust it back and strove to think of other things.

It struck him as curious that he could run at all on feet so frozen that he could not feel them when they struck the earth and took the weight of his body. He seemed to himself to skim along above the surface and to have no connection with the earth. Somewhere he had once seen a winged Mercury, and he wondered if Mercury felt as he felt when skimming over the earth.

His theory of running until he reached camp and the boys had one flaw in it: he lacked the endurance. Several times he stumbled, and finally he tottered, crumpled up, and fell. When he tried to rise, he failed. He must sit and rest, he decided, and next time he would merely walk and keep on going. As he sat and regained his breath, he noted that he was feeling quite warm and comfortable. He was not shivering, and it even seemed that a warm glow had come to his chest and trunk. And yet, when he touched his nose or cheeks, there was no sensation. Running would not thaw them out. Nor would it thaw out his hands and feet. Then the thought came to him that the frozen portions of his body must be extending. He tried to keep this thought down, to forget it, to think of something else; he was aware of the panicky feeling that it caused, and he was afraid of the panic. But the thought asserted itself, and persisted, until it produced a vision of his body totally frozen. This was too much, and he made another wild run along the trail. Once he slowed down to a walk, but the thought of the freezing extending itself made him run again.

Mercury: in ancient Roman mythology, the messenger god, often pictured
    wearing a winged cap and sandals

And all the time the dog ran with him, at his heels. When he fell down a second time, it curled its tail over its forefeet and sat in front of him facing him curiously eager and intent. The warmth and security of the animal angered him, and he cursed it till it flattened down its ears appeasingly. This time the shivering came more quickly upon the man. He was losing in his battle with the frost. It was creeping into his body from all sides. The thought of it drove him on, but he ran no more than a hundred feet, when he staggered and pitched headlong. It was his last panic. When he had recovered his breath and control, he sat up and entertained in his mind the conception of meeting death with dignity. However, the conception did not come to him in such terms. His idea of it was that he had been making a fool of himself, running around like a chicken with its head cut off—such was the simile that occurred to him. Well, he was bound to freeze anyway, and he might as well take it decently. With this newfound peace of mind came the first glimmerings of drowsiness. A good idea, he thought, to sleep off to death. It was like taking an anesthetic. Freezing was not so bad as people thought. There were lots worse ways to die.

He pictured the boys finding his body next day. Suddenly he found himself with them, coming along the trail and looking for himself. And, still with them, he came around a turn in the trail and found himself lying in the snow. He did not belong with himself any more, for even then he was out of himself, standing with the boys and looking at himself in the snow. It certainly was cold, was his thought. When he got back to the States he could tell the folks what real cold was. He drifted

---

appeasingly: in a manner intended to calm, soothe, or pacify
anesthetic: something that produces a loss of sensation

on from this to a vision of the old-timer on Sulphur Creek. He could see him quite clearly, warm and comfortable, and smoking a pipe.

"You were right, old hoss; you were right," the man mumbled to the old-timer of Sulphur Creek.

Then the man drowsed off into what seemed to him the most comfortable and satisfying sleep he had ever known. The dog sat facing him and waiting. The brief day drew to a close in a long, slow twilight. There were no signs of a fire to be made, and, besides, never in the dog's experience had it known a man to sit like that in the snow and make no fire. As the twilight drew on, its eager yearning for the fire mastered it, and with a great lifting and shifting of forefeet, it whined softly, then flattened its ears down in anticipation of being chidden by the man. But the man remained silent. Later, the dog whined loudly. And still later it crept close to the man and caught the scent of death. This made the animal bristle and back away. A little longer it delayed, howling under the stars that leaped and danced and shone brightly in the cold sky. Then it turned and trotted up the trail in the direction of the camp it knew, where were the other food providers and fire providers.

---

chidden: scolded

THE SECRET LIFE OF WALTER MITTY
by James Thurber

"We're going through!" The Commander's voice was like thin ice breaking. He wore his full-dress uniform, with the heavily braided white cap pulled down rakishly over one cold gray eye. "We can't make it, sir. It's spoiling for a hurricane, if you ask me." "I'm not asking you, Lieutenant Berg," said the Commander. "Throw on the power lights! Rev her up to 8500! We're going through!" The pounding of the cylinders increased: ta-pocketa-pocketa-pocketa-*pocketa-pocketa.* The Commander stared at the ice forming on the pilot window. He walked over and twisted a row of complicated dials. "Switch on No. 8 auxiliary!" he shouted. "Switch on No. 8 auxiliary!" repeated Lieutenant Berg. "Full strength in No. 3 turret!" shouted the Commander. "Full strength in No. 3 turret!" The crew, bending to their various tasks in the huge, hurtling eight-engined Navy hydroplane, looked at each other and grinned. "The Old Man'll get us through," they said to one another. "The Old Man ain't afraid of hell!"…

"Not so fast! You're driving too fast!" said Mrs. Mitty. "What are you driving so fast for?"

"Hmm?" said Walter Mitty. He looked at his wife, in the seat beside him, with shocked astonishment. She seemed grossly unfamiliar, like a strange woman who had yelled at him in a crowd. "You were up to fifty-five," she said. "You

---

rakishly: in a careless, jaunty way
auxiliary: a reserve or backup
turret: an armored structure that protects the gunmen on a warship
hydroplane: an airplane designed to take off from and land on water

know I don't like to go more than forty. You were up to fifty-five." Walter Mitty drove on toward Waterbury in silence, the roaring of the SN202 through the worst storm in twenty years of Navy flying fading in the remote, intimate airways of his mind. "You're tensed up again," said Mrs. Mitty. "It's one of your days. I wish you'd let Dr. Renshaw look you over."

Walter Mitty stopped the car in front of the building where his wife went to have her hair done. "Remember to get those overshoes while I'm having my hair done," she said. "I don't need overshoes," said Mitty. She put her mirror back into her bag. "We've been all through that," she said, getting out of the car. "You're not a young man any longer." He raced the engine a little. "Why don't you wear your gloves? Have you lost your gloves?" Walter Mitty reached in a pocket and brought out the gloves. He put them on, but after she had turned and gone into the building and he had driven on to a red light, he took them off again. "Pick it up, brother!" snapped a cop as the light changed, and Mitty hastily pulled on his gloves and lurched ahead. He drove around the streets aimlessly for a time, and then he drove past the hospital on his way to the parking lot.

..."It's the millionaire banker, Wellington McMillan," said the pretty nurse. "Yes?" said Walter Mitty, removing his gloves slowly. "Who has the case?" "Dr. Renshaw and Dr. Benbow, but there are two specialists here, Dr. Remington from New York and Dr. Pritchard-Mitford from London. He flew over." A door opened down a long, cool corridor and Dr. Renshaw came out. He looked distraught and haggard. "Hello, Mitty," he said. "We're having the devil's own time with McMillan, the

---

distraught: extremely upset
haggard: appearing worn out or exhausted

millionaire banker and close personal friend of Roosevelt. Obstreosis of the ductal tract. Tertiary. Wish you'd take a look at him." "Glad to," said Mitty.

In the operating room there were whispered introductions: "Dr. Remington, Dr. Mitty. Dr. Pritchard-Mitford, Dr. Mitty." "I've read your book on streptothricosis," said Pritchard-Mitford, shaking hands. "A brilliant performance, sir." "Thank you," said Walter Mitty. "Didn't know you were in the States, Mitty," grumbled Remington. "Coals to Newcastle, bringing Mitford and me up here for a tertiary." "You are very kind," said Mitty. A huge, complicated machine, connected to the operating table, with many tubes and wires, began at this moment to go pocketa-pocketa-pocketa. "The new anesthetizer is giving away!" shouted an intern. "There is no one in the East who knows how to fix it!" "Quiet, man!" said Mitty, in a low, cool voice. He sprang to the machine, which was now going pocketa-pocketa-queep-pocketa-queep. He began fingering delicately a row of glistening dials. "Give me a fountain pen!" he snapped. Someone handed him a fountain pen. He pulled a faulty piston out of the machine and inserted the pen in its place. "That will hold for ten minutes," he said. "Get on with the operation." A nurse hurried over and whispered to Renshaw, and Mitty saw the man turn pale. "Coreopsis has set in," said Renshaw

---

Roosevelt: Franklin D. Roosevelt , president of the United States from
   1933–1945
"Obstreosis of the ductal tract. Tertiary": a combination of made-up and real
   (but misused) words, here used humorously to sound like medical terms
streptothricosis: a kind of bacterial infection, usually of cattle or other
   animals, here used humorously as a medical term
"Coals to Newcastle": an expression meaning "completely unnecessary
   and pointless," since Newcastle is a coal-mining region in England
piston: a moving cylinder in a machine
Coreopsis: a kind of flower, here used humorously to sound like
   a medical term

nervously. "If you would take over, Mitty?" Mitty looked at him and at the craven figure of Benbow, who drank, and at the grave, uncertain faces of the two great specialists. "If you wish," he said. They slipped a white gown on him, he adjusted a mask and drew on thin gloves; nurses handed him shining...

"Back it up, Mac! Look out for that Buick!" Walter Mitty jammed on the brakes. "Wrong lane, Mac," said the parking-lot attendant, looking at Mitty closely. "Gee. Yeh," muttered Mitty. He began cautiously to back out of the lane marked "Exit Only." "Leave her sit there," said the attendant. "I'll put her away." Mitty got out of the car. "Hey, better leave the key." "Oh," said Mitty, handing the man the ignition key. The attendant vaulted into the car, backed it up with insolent skill, and put it where it belonged.

They're so darn cocky, thought Walter Mitty, walking along Main Street; they think they know everything. Once he had tried to take his chains off, outside New Milford, and he had got them wound around the axles. A man had had to come out in a wrecking car and unwind them, a young, grinning garageman. Since then Mrs. Mitty always made him drive to a garage to have the chains taken off. The next time, he thought, I'll wear my right arm in a sling; they won't grin at me then. I'll have my right arm in a sling and they'll see I couldn't possibly take the chains off myself. He kicked at the slush on the sidewalk. "Overshoes," he said to himself, and he began looking for a shoe store.

When he came out into the street again, with the overshoes in a box under his arm, Walter Mitty began to wonder what the other thing was his wife had told him to get. She had told him, twice before they set out from their house for Waterbury.

---

insolent: cocky; arrogant

In a way he hated these weekly trips to town—he was always getting something wrong. Kleenex, he thought. Squibb's, razor blades? No. Toothpaste, toothbrush, bicarbonate, carborundum, initiative and referendum? He gave it up. But she would remember it. "Where's the what's-its-name?" she would ask. "Don't tell me you forgot the what's-its-name." A newsboy went by shouting something about the Waterbury trial.

...."Perhaps this will refresh your memory." The District Attorney suddenly thrust a heavy automatic at the quiet figure on the witness stand. "Have you ever seen this before?" Walter Mitty took the gun and examined it expertly. "This is my Webley-Vickers 50.80," he said calmly. An excited buzz ran around the courtroom. The Judge rapped for order. "You are a crack shot with any sort of firearms, I believe?" said the District Attorney, insinuatingly. "Objection!" shouted Mitty's attorney. "We have shown that the defendant could not have fired the shot. We have shown that he wore his right arm in a sling on the night of the fourteenth of July." Walter Mitty raised his hand briefly and the bickering attorneys were stilled. "With any known make of gun," he said evenly, "I could have killed Gregory Fitzhurst at three hundred feet with my left hand." Pandemonium broke loose in the courtroom. A woman's scream rose above the bedlam and suddenly a lovely, dark-haired girl was in Walter Mitty's arms. The District Attorney struck at her savagely. Without rising from his chair, Mitty let the man have it on the point of the chin. "You miserable cur!"...

---

bicarbonate: baking soda
carborundum: a substance used for scouring or wearing down a surface
insinuatingly: in a way that casts doubt or suspicion
pandemonium: chaos; complete disorder
bedlam: a state of confusion and uproar
cur: a mongrel dog; a cowardly person

"Puppy biscuit," said Walter Mitty. He stopped walking and the buildings of Waterbury rose up out of the misty courtroom and surrounded him again. A woman who was passing laughed. "He said 'Puppy biscuit,'" she said to her companion. "That man said 'Puppy biscuit' to himself." Walter Mitty hurried on. He went into an A&P, not the first one he came to but a smaller one farther up the street. "I want some biscuit for small, young dogs," he said to the clerk. "Any special brand, sir?" The greatest pistol shot in the world thought a moment. "It says 'Puppies Bark for It' on the box," said Walter Mitty.

His wife would be through at the hairdresser's in fifteen minutes, Mitty saw in looking at his watch, unless they had trouble drying it; sometimes they had trouble drying it. She didn't like to get to the hotel first; she would want him to be there waiting for her as usual. He found a big leather chair in the lobby, facing a window, and he put the overshoes and the puppy biscuit on the floor beside it. He picked up an old copy of *Liberty* and sank down into the chair. "Can Germany Conquer the World Through the Air?" Walter Mitty looked at the pictures of bombing planes and of ruined streets.

..."The cannonading has got the wind up in young Raleigh, sir," said the sergeant. Captain Mitty looked up at him through tousled hair. "Get him to bed," he said wearily, "with the others. I'll fly alone." "But you can't, sir," said the sergeant anxiously. "It takes two men to handle that bomber and the Archies are pounding hell out of the air. Von Richtman's circus is between here and Saulier." "Somebody's

---

cannonading: heavy gunfire
tousled: disarranged; rumpled

got to get that ammunition dump," said Mitty. "I'm going over. Spot of brandy?" He poured a drink for the sergeant and one for himself. War thundered and whined around the dugout and battered at the door. There was a rending of wood and splinters flew through the room. "A bit of a near thing," said Captain Mitty carelessly. "The box barrage is closing in," said the sergeant. "We only live once, Sergeant," said Mitty, with his faint, fleeting smile. "Or do we?" He poured another brandy and tossed it off. "I never see a man could hold his brandy like you, sir," said the sergeant. "Begging your pardon, sir." Captain Mitty stood up and strapped on his huge Webley-Vickers automatic. "It's forty kilometers through hell, sir," said the sergeant. Mitty finished one last brandy. "After all," he said softly, "what isn't?" The pounding of the cannon increased; there was the rat-tat-tatting of machine guns, and from somewhere came the menacing pocketa-pocketa-pocketa of the new flame throwers. Walter Mitty walked to the door of the dugout humming "Auprès de Ma Blonde." He turned and waved to the sergeant. "Cheerio!" he said....

Something struck his shoulder. "I've been looking all over this hotel for you," said Mrs. Mitty. "Why do you have to hide in this old chair? How did you expect me to find you?" "Things close in," said Walter Mitty vaguely. "What?" Mrs. Mitty said. "Did you get the what's-its-name? The puppy biscuit? What's in that box?" "Overshoes," said Mitty. "Couldn't you have put them on in the store?" "I was thinking," said Walter Mitty. "Does it ever occur to you that I am sometimes thinking?" She looked at him. "I'm going to take your temperature when I get you home," she said.

---

barrage: heavy artillery fire

They went out through the revolving doors that made a faintly derisive whistling sound when you pushed them. It was two blocks to the parking lot. At the drugstore on the corner she said, "Wait here for me. I forgot something. I won't be a minute." She was more than a minute. Walter Mitty lighted a cigarette. It began to rain, rain with sleet in it. He stood up against the wall of the drugstore, smoking.... He put his shoulders back and his heels together. "To hell with the handkerchief," said Walter Mitty scornfully. He took one last drag on his cigarette and snapped it away. Then, with that faint, fleeting smile playing about his lips, he faced the firing squad; erect and motionless, proud and disdainful, Walter Mitty the Undefeated, inscrutable to the last.

---

derisive: mocking; expressing ridicule
disdainful: scornful; haughty
inscrutable: difficult to understand; mysterious

THE PIECE OF STRING

by Guy de Maupassant
translated by Albert M.C. McMaster and others

It was market day, and from all the country round Goderville the peasants and their wives were coming toward the town. The men walked slowly, throwing the whole body forward at every step of their long, crooked legs. They were deformed from pushing the plow, which makes the left shoulder higher, and bends their figures sideways; from reaping the grain, when they have to spread their legs so as to keep on their feet. Their starched blue blouses, glossy as though varnished, ornamented at collar and cuffs with a little embroidered design and blown out around their bony bodies, looked very much like balloons about to soar, from which issued two arms and two feet.

Some of these fellows dragged a cow or a calf at the end of a rope. And just behind the animal followed their wives, beating it over the back with a leaf-covered branch to hasten its pace, and carrying large baskets out of which protruded the heads of chickens or ducks. These women walked more quickly and energetically than the men, with their erect, dried-up figures, adorned with scanty little shawls pinned over their flat bosoms, and their heads wrapped round with a white cloth, enclosing the hair and surmounted by a cap.

Goderville: a town in northern France, in the region of Normandy
    (all towns mentioned in this story are in the same general region)
reaping: harvesting
varnished: coated with a liquid that dries to a hard, glossy surface
issued: emerged; came forth
protruded: jutted; stuck out
surmounted: topped by

Now a wagon passed by, jogging along behind a nag, strangely shaking the two men on the seat and the woman at the bottom of the cart who held fast to its sides to lessen the hard jolting.

In the marketplace at Goderville there was a great crowd, a mingled multitude of men and beasts. The horns of cattle, the high, long-napped hats of wealthy peasants, the headdresses of the women rose above the surface of that sea. And the sharp, shrill, barking voices made a continuous, wild din, while above it occasionally rose a huge burst of laughter from the sturdy lungs of a merry peasant or a prolonged bellow from a cow tied fast to the wall of a house.

It all smelled of the stable, of milk, of hay and of perspiration, giving off that half-human, half-animal odor which is peculiar to country folks.

Maître Hauchecorne, of Breaute, had just arrived at Goderville and was making his way toward the square when he perceived on the ground a little piece of string. Maître Hauchecorne, economical as are all true Normans, reflected that everything was worth picking up which could be of any use, and he stooped down, but painfully, because he suffered from rheumatism. He took the bit of thin string from the ground and was carefully preparing to roll it up when he saw Maître Malandain, the harness maker, on his doorstep staring at him. They had once had a quarrel about a halter, and they

---

nag: an old horse
din: noise
Maître: French title meaning "Master"
Normans: the inhabitants of Normandy, in northern France
rheumatism: achy bones and muscles

had borne each other malice ever since. Maître Hauchecorne was overcome with a sort of shame at being seen by his enemy picking up a bit of string in the road. He quickly hid it beneath his blouse and then slipped it into his breeches pocket, then pretended to be still looking for something on the ground which he did not discover and finally went off toward the marketplace, his head bent forward and his body almost doubled in two by rheumatic pains.

He was at once lost in the crowd, which kept moving about slowly and noisily as it chaffered and bargained. The peasants examined the cows, went off, came back, always in doubt for fear of being cheated, never quite daring to decide, looking the seller square in the eye in the effort to discover the tricks of the man and the defect in the beast.

The women, having placed their great baskets at their feet, had taken out the poultry, which lay upon the ground, their legs tied together, with terrified eyes and scarlet combs.

They listened to propositions, maintaining their prices in a decided manner with an impassive face or perhaps deciding to accept the smaller price offered, suddenly calling out to the customer who was starting to go away, "All right, I'll let you have them, Maître Anthime."

Then, little by little, the square became empty, and when the Angelus struck midday those who lived at a distance poured into the inns.

At Jourdain's the great room was filled with eaters, just as the vast court was filled with vehicles of every sort—carts,

---

malice: ill will; the desire to see another come to harm
breeches: pants
chaffered: haggled; bargained
impassive: expressionless; blank
Angelus: a bell rung in Catholic churches three times a day to call people
    to prayer

gigs, wagons, tilburies, innumerable vehicles which have no name, yellow with mud, misshapen, pieced together, raising their shafts to heaven like two arms, or it may be with their nose on the ground and their rear in the air.

Just opposite the diners seated at the table, the huge fireplace, with its bright flame, gave out a burning heat on the backs of those who sat at the right. Three spits were turning, loaded with chickens, with pigeons and with joints of mutton; and a delectable odor of roast meat and of gravy flowing over crisp brown skin arose from the hearth, kindled merriment, and caused every mouth to water.

All the aristocracy of the plow were eating there at Maître Jourdain's, the innkeeper's, a dealer in horses also and a sharp fellow who had made a great deal of money in his day.

The dishes were passed round and emptied, as were the jugs of yellow cider. Everyone told of his affairs, of his purchases and his sales. They exchanged news about the crops. The weather was good for greens, but too wet for grain.

Suddenly the drum began to beat in the courtyard before the house. All except the most indifferent were on their feet at once and ran to the door, to the windows, their mouths full and napkins in hand.

When the public crier had finished his drum-beating, he called forth in a jerky voice, pausing in the wrong places:

"Be it known to the inhabitants of Goderville and in general to all persons present at the market that there has been lost this morning on the Benzeville road, between nine and ten o'clock, a black leather pocketbook containing five hundred francs and business papers. The finder is requested to return it to the

---

tilburies: two-seat carriages
francs: French money

mayor's office at once or to Maître Fortune Houlbreque of Manneville. There will be twenty francs reward."

Then the man went away. They heard once more at a distance the dull beating of the drum and the faint voice of the crier. Then they all began to talk of this incident, reckoning up the chances which Maître Houlbreque had of finding or of not finding his pocketbook again.

The meal went on. They were finishing their coffee when the corporal of gendarmes appeared on the threshold.

He asked, "Is Maître Hauchecorne of Breaute here?"

Maître Hauchecorne, seated at the other end of the table, answered, "Here I am."

The officer responded, "Maître Hauchecorne, will you be so good as to accompany me to the mayor's office. The mayor would like to talk with you."

The peasant, surprised, swallowed his tiny glass of brandy, rose, and, even more bent than in the morning, for the first steps after each rest were especially difficult, set out, repeating, "Here I am, here I am."

The mayor was waiting for him, seated in an armchair. He was the notary of the place, a stout, grave man of pompous speech.

"Maître Hauchecorne," said he, "this morning on the Benzeville road, you were seen picking up the pocketbook lost by Maître Houlbreque, of Manneville."

The countryman looked at the mayor in amazement, frightened already at this suspicion which rested on him, he knew not why.

_____

gendarmes: the French police force
notary: a public officer who is responsible for such tasks as verifying
  official documents
pompous: self-important; pretentious

"Me? Me? Me pick up the pocketbook?"

"Yes, you."

"I swear I don't even know anything about it."

"You were seen."

"I was seen—me? Who says he saw me?"

"Monsieur Malandain, the harness-maker."

Then the old man remembered, understood, and, reddening with anger, said, "Ah! he saw me, did he, the rascal? He saw me picking up this string here, M'sieu the Mayor."

And fumbling at the bottom of his pocket, he pulled out of it the little end of string.

But the mayor incredulously shook his head: "You will not make me believe, Maître Hauchecorne, that Monsieur Malandain, who is a man whose word can be relied on, has mistaken this string for a pocketbook."

The peasant, furious, raised his hand and spat on the ground beside him as if to attest his good faith, repeating, "For all that, it is God's truth, M'sieu the Mayor. There! On my soul's salvation, I repeat it."

The mayor continued: "After you picked up the object in question, you even looked about for some time in the mud to see if a piece of money had not dropped out of it."

The good man was choking with indignation and fear. "How can they tell—how can they tell such lies as that to slander an honest man! How can they?"

His protestations were in vain; he was not believed.

He was confronted with Monsieur Malandain, who repeated

M'sieu: Monsieur (French for "Mister")
incredulously: with disbelief
indignation: anger caused by something unjust
slander: false statements made to injure someone

and sustained his testimony. They railed at one another for an hour. At his own request Maître Hauchecorne was searched. Nothing was found on him.

At last the mayor, much perplexed, sent him away, warning him that he would inform the public prosecutor and ask for orders.

The news had spread. When he left the mayor's office the old man was surrounded, interrogated with a curiosity which was serious or mocking, as the case might be, but into which no indignation entered. And he began to tell the story of the string. They did not believe him. They laughed at him.

He passed on, buttonholed by every one, himself buttonholing his acquaintances, beginning over and over again his tale and his protestations, showing his pockets turned inside out to prove that he had nothing in them.

They said to him: "You old rogue!"

He grew more and more angry, feverish, in despair at not being believed, and kept on telling his story.

The night came. It was time to go home. He left with three of his neighbors, to whom he pointed out the place where he had picked up the string, and all the way he talked of his adventure.

That evening he made the round of the village of Breaute for the purpose of telling every one. He met only unbelievers.

He felt ill about it all night long.

The next day, about one in the afternoon, Marius Paumelle, a farm hand of Maître Breton, the market gardener at Ymanville, returned the pocketbook and its contents to Maître Holbreque of Manneville.

---

railed: yelled angrily
buttonholed: detained in conversation
rogue: a scoundrel; an unprincipled person

This man said, indeed, that he had found it on the road, but not knowing how to read, he had carried it home and given it to his master.

The news spread through the neighborhood. Maître Hauchecorne was informed. He started off at once and began to relate his story with the denouement. He was triumphant.

"What grieved me," said he, "was not the thing itself, do you understand, but it was being accused of lying. Nothing does you so much harm as being in disgrace for lying."

All day he talked of his adventure. He told it on the roads to the people who passed, at the wineshop to the people drinking there, and next Sunday when they came out of church. He even stopped strangers to tell them about it. He was easy now, and yet something worried him without his knowing exactly what it was. People had a joking manner while they listened. They did not seem convinced. He seemed to feel their remarks behind his back.

On Tuesday of the following week he went to market at Goderville, prompted solely by the need of telling his story.

Malandain, standing on his doorstep, began to laugh as he saw him pass. Why?

He approached a farmer of Criquetot, who did not let him finish, and giving him a punch in the pit of the stomach cried in his face, "Oh, you great rogue!" Then he turned his heel upon him.

Maître Hauchecorne remained speechless and grew more and more uneasy. Why was he called a "great rogue"?

When seated at table in Jourdain's tavern he began again to explain the whole affair.

denouement: the final outcome of a story

A horse dealer of Montivilliers shouted at him, "Get out, get out, you old scamp! I know all about your old string."

Hauchecorne stammered, "But since they found it again, the pocketbook!"

But the other continued, "Hold your tongue, old one; there's one who finds it and there's another who returns it. And no one the wiser."

The farmer was speechless. He understood at last. They accused him of having had the pocketbook brought back by an accomplice, by a confederate.

He tried to protest. The whole table began to laugh.

He could not finish his dinner, and went away amid a chorus of jeers.

He went home indignant, choking with rage, with confusion, the more cast down since with his Norman craftiness he was, perhaps, capable of having done what they accused him of and even of boasting of it as a good trick. He was dimly conscious that it was impossible to prove his innocence, his craftiness being so well known. He felt himself struck to the heart by the injustice of the suspicion.

He began anew to tell his tale, lengthening his recital every day, each day adding new proofs, more energetic declarations and more sacred oaths, which he thought of and prepared in his hours of solitude, for his mind was entirely occupied with the story of the string. The more he denied it, the more complicated his arguments, the less he was believed.

"Those are liars' proofs," they said behind his back.

He felt this. It preyed upon him and he exhausted himself in useless efforts.

---

scamp: a rascal
confederate: a partner

He was visibly wasting away.

Jokers would make him tell the story of "the piece of string" to amuse them, just as you make a soldier who has been on a campaign tell his story of the battle. His mind kept growing weaker, and about the end of December he took to his bed.

He passed away early in January, and, in the ravings of death agony, he protested his innocence, repeating: "A little bit of string—a little bit of string. See, here it is, M'sieu the Mayor."

THE TELL-TALE HEART
by Edgar Allan Poe

True! nervous—very, very dreadfully nervous I had been and am; but why *will* you say that I am mad? The disease had sharpened my senses—not destroyed—not dulled them. Above all was the sense of hearing acute. I heard all things in the heaven and in the earth. I heard many things in hell. How, then, am I mad? Hearken! and observe how healthily— how calmly I can tell you the whole story.

It is impossible to say how first the idea entered my brain; but once conceived, it haunted me day and night. Object there was none. Passion there was none. I loved the old man. He had never wronged me. He had never given me insult. For his gold I had no desire. I think it was his eye! yes, it was this! He had the eye of a vulture—a pale blue eye, with a film over it. Whenever it fell upon me, my blood ran cold; and so by degrees—very gradually—I made up my mind to take the life of the old man, and thus rid myself of the eye forever.

Now this is the point. You fancy *me* mad. Madmen know nothing. But you should have seen me. You should have seen how wisely I proceeded—with what caution—with what foresight—with what dissimulation I went to work! I was never kinder to the old man than during the whole week

mad: insane
acute: sharp; keen; extremely perceptive
hearken: listen
object: a goal
passion: powerful emotion
fancy: to imagine; to suppose
dissimulation: deception; concealment of one's true intentions

before I killed him. And every night, about midnight, I turned the latch of his door and opened it—oh so gently! And then, when I had made an opening sufficient for my head, I put in a dark lantern, all closed, closed, that no light shone out, and then I thrust in my head. Oh, you would have laughed to see how cunningly I thrust it in! I moved it slowly—very, very slowly, so that I might not disturb the old man's sleep. It took me an hour to place my whole head within the opening so far that I could see him as he lay upon his bed. Ha!—would a madman have been so wise as this? And then, when my head was well in the room, I undid the lantern cautiously—oh, so cautiously—cautiously (for the hinges creaked)—I undid it just so much that a single thin ray fell upon the vulture eye. And this I did for seven long nights—every night just at midnight—but I found the eye always closed; and so it was impossible to do the work; for it was not the old man who vexed me, but his Evil Eye. And every morning, when the day broke, I went boldly into the chamber, and spoke courageously to him, calling him by name in a hearty tone, and inquiring how he had passed the night. So you see he would have been a very profound old man, indeed, to suspect that every night, just at twelve, I looked in upon him while he slept.

Upon the eighth night I was more than usually cautious in opening the door. A watch's minute hand moves more quickly than did mine. Never before that night had I *felt* the extent of my own powers—of my sagacity. I could scarcely contain my feelings of triumph. To think that there I was, opening the door,

---

cunningly: deceptively
vexed: troubled; distressed
sagacity: wisdom; keen judgment and understanding

little by little, and he not even to dream of my secret deeds or thoughts. I fairly chuckled at the idea; and perhaps he heard me; for he moved on the bed suddenly, as if startled. Now you may think that I drew back—but no. His room was as black as pitch with the thick darkness (for the shutters were close fastened, through fear of robbers), and so I knew that he could not see the opening of the door, and I kept pushing it on steadily, steadily.

I had my head in, and was about to open the lantern, when my thumb slipped upon the tin fastening, and the old man sprang up in bed, crying out, "Who's there?"

I kept quite still and said nothing. For a whole hour I did not move a muscle, and in the meantime I did not hear him lie down. He was still sitting up in the bed listening—just as I have done, night after night, hearkening to the death watches in the wall.

Presently I heard a slight groan, and I knew it was the groan of mortal terror. It was not a groan of pain or of grief—oh, no!—it was the low stifled sound that arises from the bottom of the soul when overcharged with awe. I knew the sound well. Many a night, just at midnight, when all the world slept, it has welled up from my own bosom, deepening, with its dreadful echo, the terrors that distracted me. I say I knew it well. I knew what the old man felt, and pitied him, although I chuckled at heart. I knew that he had been lying awake ever since the first slight noise, when he had turned in the bed. His fears had been ever since growing upon him. He had been trying to fancy them causeless, but could not. He had been saying to himself—"It is nothing but the wind in the chimney—it is only a mouse crossing the floor," or "It is merely a cricket which has made

_____

overcharged: filled to overflowing

a single chirp." Yes, he had been trying to comfort himself with these suppositions: but he had found all in vain. *All in vain;* because Death, in approaching him, had stalked with his black shadow before him, and enveloped the victim. And it was the mournful influence of the unperceived shadow that caused him to feel—although he neither saw nor heard—to *feel* the presence of my head within the room.

When I had waited a long time, very patiently, without hearing him lie down, I resolved to open a little—a very, very little crevice in the lantern. So I opened it—you cannot imagine how stealthily, stealthily—until, at length a simple dim ray, like the thread of the spider, shot from out the crevice and fell full upon the vulture eye.

It was open—wide, wide open—and I grew furious as I gazed upon it. I saw it with perfect distinctiveness—all a dull blue, with a hideous veil over it that chilled the very marrow in my bones; but I could see nothing else of the old man's face or person: for I had directed the ray as if by instinct, precisely upon the damned spot.

And have I not told you that what you mistake for madness is but overacuteness of the senses?—now, I say, there came to my ears a low, dull, quick sound, such as a watch makes when enveloped in cotton. I knew *that* sound well, too. It was the beating of the old man's heart. It increased my fury, as the beating of a drum stimulates the soldier into courage.

But even yet I refrained and kept still. I scarcely breathed. I held the lantern motionless. I tried how steadily I could

---

suppositions: assumptions; beliefs without evidence
enveloped: enclosed; surrounded totally
crevice: a narrow opening or crack
stealthily: in a cautious, secretive way
distinctiveness: clarity

maintain the ray upon the eye. Meantime the hellish tattoo of the heart increased. It grew quicker and quicker, and louder and louder every instant. The old man's terror *must* have been extreme! It grew louder, I say, louder every moment!— do you mark me well? I have told you that I am nervous: so I am. And now at the dead hour of the night, amid the dreadful silence of that old house, so strange a noise as this excited me to uncontrollable terror. Yet, for some minutes longer I refrained and stood still. But the beating grew louder, louder! I thought the heart must burst. And now a new anxiety seized me—the sound would be heard by a neighbor! The old man's hour had come! With a loud yell, I threw open the lantern and leaped into the room. He shrieked once—once only. In an instant I dragged him to the floor, and pulled the heavy bed over him. I then smiled gaily, to find the deed so far done. But, for many minutes, the heart beat on with a muffled sound. This, however, did not vex me; it would not be heard through the wall. At length it ceased. The old man was dead. I removed the bed and examined the corpse. Yes, he was stone, stone dead. I placed my hand upon the heart and held it there many minutes. There was no pulsation. He was stone dead. His eye would trouble me no more.

If still you think me mad, you will think so no longer when I describe the wise precautions I took for the concealment of the body. The night waned, and I worked hastily, but in silence. First of all I dismembered the corpse. I cut off the head and the arms and the legs.

---

tattoo: a rhythmic tapping sound, as of a drum
pulsation: beating; throbbing
waned: decreased; approached an end

I then took up three planks from the flooring of the chamber, and deposited all between the scantlings. I then replaced the boards so cleverly, so cunningly, that no human eye—not even *his*—could have detected anything wrong. There was nothing to wash out—no stain of any kind—no blood spot whatever. I had been too wary for that. A tub had caught all—ha! ha!

When I had made an end of these labors, it was four o'clock—still dark as midnight. As the bell sounded the hour, there came a knocking at the street door. I went down to open it with a light heart—for what had I *now* to fear? There entered three men, who introduced themselves, with perfect suavity, as officers of the police. A shriek had been heard by a neighbor during the night; suspicion of foul play had been aroused; information had been lodged at the police office, and they (the officers) had been deputed to search the premises.

I smiled—for *what* had I to fear? I bade the gentlemen welcome. The shriek, I said, was my own in a dream. The old man, I mentioned, was absent in the country. I took my visitors all over the house. I bade them search—search *well*. I led them, at length, to *his* chamber. I showed them his treasures, secure, undisturbed. In the enthusiasm of my confidence, I brought chairs into the room, and desired them *here* to rest from their fatigues, while I myself, in the wild audacity of my perfect triumph, placed my own seat upon the very spot beneath which reposed the corpse of the victim.

The officers were satisfied. My *manner* had convinced them. I was singularly at ease. They sat, and while I answered

scantlings: small pieces of lumber
suavity: pleasantness; politeness
audacity: reckless, daring boldness
reposed: lay at rest

cheerily, they chatted of familiar things. But, erelong, I felt myself getting pale and wished them gone. My head ached, and I fancied a ringing in my ears: but still they sat and still chatted. The ringing became more distinct—it continued and became more distinct; I talked more freely to get rid of the feeling; but it continued and gained definiteness—until, at length, I found that the noise was *not* within my ears.

No doubt I now grew *very* pale;—but I talked more fluently, and with a heightened voice. Yet the sound increased—and what could I do? It was a *low, dull, quick sound—much such a sound as a watch makes when enveloped in cotton.* I gasped for breath—and yet the officers heard it not. I talked more quickly—more vehemently; but the noise steadily increased. I arose and argued about trifles, in a high key and with violent gesticulations; but the noise steadily increased. Why *would* they not be gone? I paced the floor to and fro with heavy strides, as if excited to fury by the observations of the men—but the noise steadily increased. Oh God! what *could* I do? I foamed—I raved—I swore! I swung the chair upon which I had been sitting, and grated it upon the boards, but the noise arose over all and continually increased. It grew louder—louder—*louder!* And still the men chatted pleasantly, and smiled. Was it possible they heard not? Almighty God!—no, no! They heard!—they suspected!— they *knew!*—they were making a mockery of my horror!— this I thought, and this I think. But anything was better than this agony! Anything was more tolerable than this

_____

erelong: soon
fluently: smoothly; in an effortless, flowing manner
vehemently: forcefully; with strong emotion
trifles: unimportant things
gesticulations: excited and forceful gestures

derision! I could bear those hypocritical smiles no longer!
I felt that I must scream or die! and now—again!—hark!
louder! louder! louder! *louder!*

"Villains!" I shrieked, "dissemble no more! I admit the
deed!—tear up the planks! here, here!—it is the beating of
his hideous heart!"

---

derision: scorn
hypocritical: false; deceptive; showing or saying one thing but
    meaning another
dissemble: to deceive; to conceal

THE LOTTERY
by Shirley Jackson

The morning of June 27th was clear and sunny, with the fresh warmth of a full-summer day; the flowers were blossoming profusely and the grass was richly green. The people of the village began to gather in the square, between the post office and the bank, around ten o'clock; in some towns there were so many people that the lottery took two days and had to be started on June 26th, but in this village, where there were only about three hundred people, the whole lottery took less than two hours, so it could begin at ten o'clock in the morning and still be through in time to allow the villagers to get home for noon dinner.

The children assembled first, of course. School was recently over for the summer, and the feeling of liberty sat uneasily on most of them; they tended to gather together quietly for a while before they broke into boisterous play, and their talk was still of the classroom and the teacher, of books and reprimands. Bobby Martin had already stuffed his pockets full of stones, and the other boys soon followed his example, selecting the smoothest and roundest stones; Bobby and Harry Jones and Dickie Delacroix—the villagers pronounced this name "Dellacroy"— eventually made a great pile of stones in one corner of the square and guarded it against the raids of the other boys. The girls stood aside, talking among themselves, looking over their

---

profusely: abundantly; in great amounts
boisterous: noisy and rowdy
reprimands: sharp criticisms; severe scoldings

shoulders at the boys, and the very small children rolled in the dust or clung to the hands of their older brothers or sisters.

Soon the men began to gather, surveying their own children, speaking of planting and rain, tractors and taxes. They stood together, away from the pile of stones in the corner, and their jokes were quiet and they smiled rather than laughed. The women, wearing faded house dresses and sweaters, came shortly after their menfolk. They greeted one another and exchanged bits of gossip as they went to join their husbands. Soon the women, standing by their husbands, began to call to their children, and the children came reluctantly, having to be called four or five times. Bobby Martin ducked under his mother's grasping hand and ran, laughing, back to the pile of stones. His father spoke up sharply, and Bobby came quickly and took his place between his father and his oldest brother.

The lottery was conducted—as were the square dances, the teen-age club, the Halloween program—by Mr. Summers, who had time and energy to devote to civic activities. He was a round-faced, jovial man and he ran the coal business, and people were sorry for him, because he had no children and his wife was a scold. When he arrived in the square, carrying the black wooden box, there was a murmur of conversation among the villagers, and he waved and called, "Little late today, folks." The postmaster, Mr. Graves, followed him, carrying a three-legged stool, and the stool was put in the center of the square and Mr. Summers set the black box down on it. The villagers kept their distance, leaving a space between themselves and the stool, and when Mr. Summers

---

surveying: watching over
scold: one who habitually nags and criticizes

141

said, "Some of you fellows want to give me a hand?" there was a hesitation before two men, Mr. Martin and his oldest son, Baxter, came forward to hold the box steady on the stool while Mr. Summers stirred up the papers inside it.

The original paraphernalia for the lottery had been lost long ago, and the black box now resting on the stool had been put into use even before Old Man Warner, the oldest man in town, was born. Mr. Summers spoke frequently to the villagers about making a new box, but no one liked to upset even as much tradition as was represented by the black box. There was a story that the present box had been made with some pieces of the box that had preceded it, the one that had been constructed when the first people settled down to make a village here. Every year, after the lottery, Mr. Summers began talking again about a new box, but every year the subject was allowed to fade off without anything's being done. The black box grew shabbier each year; by now it was no longer completely black but splintered badly along one side to show the original wood color, and in some places faded or stained.

Mr. Martin and his oldest son, Baxter, held the black box securely on the stool until Mr. Summers had stirred the papers thoroughly with his hand. Because so much of the ritual had been forgotten or discarded, Mr. Summers had been successful in having slips of paper substituted for the chips of wood that had been used for generations. Chips of wood, Mr. Summers had argued, had been all very well when the village was tiny, but now that the population was more than three hundred and likely to keep on growing, it was necessary to use something that would fit more easily into the black box. The night before the lottery, Mr. Summers and Mr. Graves

paraphernalia: equipment; items needed for a task

made up the slips of paper and put them in the box, and it was then taken to the safe of Mr. Summers's coal company and locked up until Mr. Summers was ready to take it to the square next morning. The rest of the year, the box was put away, sometimes one place, sometimes another: it had spent one year in Mr. Graves's barn and another year underfoot in the post office, and sometimes it was set on a shelf in the Martin grocery and left there.

There was a great deal of fussing to be done before Mr. Summers declared the lottery open. There were the lists to make up—of heads of families, heads of households in each family, members of each household in each family. There was the proper swearing-in of Mr. Summers by the postmaster, as the official of the lottery; at one time, some people remembered, there had been a recital of some sort, performed by the official of the lottery, a perfunctory, tuneless chant that had been rattled off duly each year; some people believed that the official of the lottery used to stand just so when he said or sang it, others believed that he was supposed to walk among the people, but years and years ago this part of the ritual had been allowed to lapse. There had been, also, a ritual salute, which the official of the lottery had had to use in addressing each person who came up to draw from the box, but this also changed with time, until now it was felt necessary only for the official to speak to each person approaching. Mr. Summers was very good at all this; in his clean white shirt and blue jeans, with one hand resting carelessly on the black box, he seemed very proper and important as he talked interminably to Mr. Graves and the Martins.

---

perfunctory: indifferent; routine; done in a careless, inattentive, hasty way
interminably: seemingly endless; wearisome

Just as Mr. Summers finally left off talking and turned to the assembled villagers, Mrs. Hutchinson came hurriedly along the path to the square, her sweater thrown over her shoulders, and slid into place in the back of the crowd. "Clean forgot what day it was," she said to Mrs. Delacroix, who stood next to her, and they both laughed softly. "Thought my old man was out back stacking wood," Mrs. Hutchinson went on, "and then I looked out the window and the kids was gone, and then I remembered it was the twenty-seventh and came a-running." She dried her hands on her apron, and Mrs. Delacroix said, "You're in time though. They're still talking away up there."

Mrs. Hutchinson craned her neck to see through the crowd and found her husband and children standing near the front. She tapped Mrs. Delacroix on the arm as a farewell and began to make her way through the crowd, "Here comes your Missus, Hutchinson," and "Bill, she made it after all." Mrs. Hutchinson reached her husband, and Mr. Summers, who had been waiting, said cheerfully, "Thought we were going to have to get on without you, Tessie." Mrs. Hutchinson said, grinning, "Wouldn't have me leave m'dishes in the sink, now, would you Joe?" and soft laughter ran through the crowd as the people stirred back into position after Mrs. Hutchinson's arrival.

"Well, now," Mr. Summers said soberly, "guess we better get started, get this over with, so's we can go back to work. Anybody ain't here?"

"Dunbar," several people said. "Dunbar, Dunbar."

Mr. Summers consulted his list. "Clyde Dunbar," he said. "That's right. He's broke his leg, hasn't he. Who's drawing for him?"

"Me, I guess," a woman said, and Mr. Summers turned to look at her. "Wife draws for her husband," Mr. Summers said. "Don't you have a grown boy to do it for you, Janey?"

Although Mr. Summers and everyone else in the village knew the answer perfectly well, it was the business of the official of the lottery to ask such questions formally. Mr. Summers waited with an expression of polite interest while Mrs. Dunbar answered.

"Horace's not but sixteen yet," Mrs. Dunbar said regretfully. "Guess I gotta fill in for the old man this year."

"Right," Mr. Summers said. He made a note on the list he was holding. Then he asked, "Watson boy drawing this year?"

A tall boy in the crowd raised his hand. "Here," he said. "I'm drawing for m'mother and me." He blinked his eyes nervously and ducked his head as several voices in the crowd said things like "Good fellow, Jack," and "Glad to see your mother's got a man to do it."

"Well," Mr. Summers said, "guess that's everyone. Old Man Warner make it?"

"Here," a voice said, and Mr. Summers nodded.

A sudden hush fell on the crowd as Mr. Summers cleared his throat and looked at the list. "All ready?" he called. "Now, I'll read the names—heads of families first—and the men come up and take a paper out of the box. Keep the paper folded in your hand without looking at it until everyone has had a turn. Everything clear?"

The people had done it so many times that they only half listened to the directions; most of them were quiet, wetting their lips, not looking around. Then Mr. Summers raised one hand high and said, "Adams." A man disengaged himself from the crowd and came forward. "Hi, Steve," Mr. Summers said, and Mr. Adams said, "Hi, Joe." They grinned at one another humorlessly and nervously. Then Mr. Adams reached into the black box and took out a folded paper. He held it firmly by one corner as he turned and went hastily back to his place in the crowd, where he stood a little apart from his family, not looking down at his hand.

"Allen," Mr. Summers said. "Anderson. . . . Bentham."

"Seems like there's no time at all between lotteries any more," Mrs. Delacroix said to Mrs. Graves in the back row. "Seems like we got through with the last one only last week."

"Time sure goes fast," Mrs. Graves said.

"Clark. . . . Delacroix."

"There goes my old man," Mrs. Delacroix said. She held her breath while her husband went forward.

"Dunbar," Mr. Summers said, and Mrs. Dunbar went steadily to the box while one of the women said, "Go on, Janey," and another said, "There she goes."

"We're next," Mrs. Graves said. She watched while Mr. Graves came around from the side of the box, greeted Mr. Summers gravely, and selected a slip of paper from the box. By now, all through the crowd there were men holding the small folded papers in their large hands, turning them over and over nervously. Mrs. Dunbar and her two sons stood together, Mrs. Dunbar holding the slip of paper.

"Harburt. . . . Hutchinson."

"Get up there, Bill," Mrs. Hutchinson said, and the people near her laughed.

"Jones."

"They do say," Mr. Adams said to Old Man Warner, who stood next to him, "that over in the north village they're talking of giving up the lottery."

Old Man Warner snorted. "Pack of crazy fools," he said. "Listening to the young folks, nothing's good enough for *them.* Next thing you know, they'll be wanting to go back to living in caves, nobody work any more, live *that* way for a while. Used to be a saying about 'Lottery in June, corn be heavy soon.' First thing you know, we'd all be eating stewed chickweed and acorns. There's *always* been a lottery," he added petulantly. "Bad enough to see young Joe Summers up there joking with everybody."

"Some places have already quit lotteries," Mrs. Adams said.

"Nothing but trouble in *that*," Old Man Warner said stoutly. "Pack of young fools."

"Martin." And Bobby Martin watched his father go forward. "Overdyke. . . . Percy."

"I wish they'd hurry," Mrs. Dunbar said to her oldest son. "I wish they'd hurry."

"They're almost through," her son said.

"You get ready to run tell Dad," Mrs. Dunbar said.

Mr. Summers called his own name and then stepped forward precisely and selected a slip from the box. Then he called, "Warner."

"Seventy-seventh year I been in the lottery," Old Man Warner said as he went through the crowd. "Seventy-seventh time."

"Watson." The tall boy came awkwardly through the crowd. Someone said, "Don't be nervous, Jack," and Mr. Summers said, "Take your time, son."

"Zanini."

After that, there was a long pause, a breathless pause, until Mr. Summers, holding his slip of paper in the air, said, "All right, fellows." For a minute, no one moved, and then all the slips of paper were opened. Suddenly, all the women began to speak at once, saying, "Who is it?" "Who's got it?" "Is it the Dunbars?" "Is it the Watsons?" Then the voices began to say, "It's Hutchinson. It's Bill." "Bill Hutchinson's got it."

---

petulantly: irritably; with ill temper

"Go tell your father," Mrs. Dunbar said to her older son.

People began to look around to see the Hutchinsons. Bill Hutchinson was standing quiet, staring down at the paper in his hand. Suddenly, Tessie Hutchinson shouted to Mr. Summers, "You didn't give him time enough to take any paper he wanted. I saw you. It wasn't fair!"

"Be a good sport, Tessie," Mrs. Delacroix called, and Mrs. Graves said, "All of us took the same chance."

"Shut up, Tessie," Bill Hutchinson said.

"Well, everyone," Mr. Summers said, "that was done pretty fast, and now we've got to be hurrying a little more to get done in time." He consulted his next list. "Bill," he said, "you draw for the Hutchinson family. You got any other households in the Hutchinsons?"

"There's Don and Eva," Mrs. Hutchinson yelled. "Make them take their chance!"

"Daughters draw with their husbands' families, Tessie," Mr. Summers said gently. "You know that as well as anyone else."

"It wasn't *fair*," Tessie said.

"I guess not, Joe," Bill Hutchinson said regretfully. "My daughter draws with her husband's family, that's only fair. And I've got no other family except the kids."

"Then, as far as drawing for families is concerned, it's you," Mr. Summers said in explanation, "and as far as drawing for households is concerned, that's you, too. Right?"

"Right," Bill Hutchinson said.

"How many kids, Bill?" Mr. Summers asked formally.

"Three," Bill Hutchinson said. "There's Bill, Jr., and Nancy, and little Dave. And Tessie and me."

"All right, then," Mr. Summers said. "Harry, you got their tickets back?"

Mr. Graves nodded and held up the slips of paper. "Put them in the box, then," Mr. Summers directed. "Take Bill's and put it in."

"I think we ought to start over," Mrs. Hutchinson said, as quietly as she could. "I tell you it wasn't *fair*. You didn't give him time enough to choose. Everybody saw that."

Mr. Graves had selected the five slips and put them in the box, and he dropped all the papers but those onto the ground, where the breeze caught them and lifted them off.

"Listen, everybody," Mrs. Hutchinson was saying to the people around her.

"Ready, Bill?" Mr. Summers asked, and Bill Hutchinson, with one quick glance around at his wife and children, nodded.

"Remember," Mr. Summers said, "take the slips and keep them folded until each person has taken one. Harry, you help little Dave." Mr. Graves took the hand of the little boy, who came willingly with him up to the box. "Take a paper out of the box, Davy," Mr. Summers said. Davy put his hand into the box and laughed. "Take just *one* paper," Mr. Summers said. "Harry, you hold it for him." Mr. Graves took the child's hand and removed the folded paper from the tight fist and held it while little Dave stood next to him and looked up at him wonderingly.

"Nancy next," Mr. Summers said. Nancy was twelve, and her school friends breathed heavily as she went forward, switching her skirt, and took a slip daintily from the box. "Bill, Jr.," Mr. Summers said, and Billy, his face red and his feet overlarge, nearly knocked the box over as he got a paper out. "Tessie," Mr. Summers said. She hesitated for a minute, looking around defiantly, and then set her lips and went up to the box. She snatched a paper out and held it behind her.

"Bill," Mr. Summers said, and Bill Hutchinson reached into the box and felt around, bringing his hand out at last with the slip of paper in it.

The crowd was quiet. A girl whispered, "I hope it's not Nancy," and the sound of the whisper reached the edges of the crowd.

"It's not the way it used to be," Old Man Warner said clearly. "People ain't the way they used to be."

"All right," Mr. Summers said, "Open the papers. Harry, you open little Dave's."

Mr. Graves opened the slip of paper and there was a general sigh through the crowd as he held it up and everyone could see that it was blank. Nancy and Bill, Jr., opened theirs at the same time, and both beamed and laughed, turning around to the crowd and holding their slips of paper above their heads.

"Tessie," Mr. Summers said. There was a pause, and then Mr. Summers looked at Bill Hutchinson, and Bill unfolded his paper and showed it. It was blank.

"It's Tessie," Mr. Summers said, and his voice was hushed. "Show us her paper, Bill."

Bill Hutchinson went over to his wife and forced the slip of paper out of her hand. It had a black spot on it, the black spot Mr. Summers had made the night before with the heavy pencil in the coal-company office. Bill Hutchinson held it up, and there was a stir in the crowd. "All right, folks," Mr. Summers said. "Let's finish quickly."

Although the villagers had forgotten the ritual and lost the original black box, they still remembered to use stones. The pile of stones the boys had made earlier was ready; there were stones on the ground with the blowing scraps of paper that had come out of the box. Mrs. Delacroix selected a stone so large she had to pick it up with both hands and turned to Mrs. Dunbar. "Come on," she said. "Hurry up."

Mrs. Dunbar had small stones in both hands, and she said, gasping for breath, "I can't run at all. You'll have to go ahead and I'll catch up with you."

The children had stones already, and someone gave little Davy Hutchinson a few pebbles.

Tessie Hutchinson was in the center of a cleared space by now, and she held her hands out desperately as the villagers moved in on her. "It isn't fair," she said. A stone hit her on the side of the head.

Old Man Warner was saying, "Come on, come on, everyone." Steve Adams was in the front of the crowd of villagers, with Mrs. Graves beside him.

"It isn't fair, it isn't right," Mrs. Hutchinson screamed, and then they were upon her.

THE LADY OR THE TIGER?
by Frank R. Stockton

In the very olden time, there lived a semi-barbaric king, whose ideas, though somewhat polished and sharpened by the progressiveness of distant Latin neighbors, were still large, florid, and untrammeled, as became the half of him which was barbaric. He was a man of exuberant fancy, and, withal, of an authority so irresistible that, at his will, he turned his varied fancies into facts. He was greatly given to self-communing, and, when he and himself agreed upon anything, the thing was done. When every member of his domestic and political systems moved smoothly in its appointed course, his nature was bland and genial; but, whenever there was a little hitch, and some of his orbs got out of their orbits, he was blander and more genial still, for nothing pleased him so much as to make the crooked straight and crush down uneven places.

Among the borrowed notions by which his barbarism had become semified was that of the public arena, in which, by exhibitions of manly and beastly valor, the minds of his subjects were refined and cultured.

---

semi-barbaric: partially uncivilized
florid: overly elaborate; marked by emotional intensity
untrammeled: not limited or restricted
exuberant: unrestrained; extreme; bursting with enthusiasm
withal: besides; also
fancies: interests; tastes
self-communing: consulting one's own thoughts; talking to oneself
genial: friendly
orbs: spheres; planets
semified: cut in half; reduced
valor: bravery

But even here the exuberant and barbaric fancy asserted itself. The arena of the king was built, not to give the people an opportunity of hearing the rhapsodies of dying gladiators, nor to enable them to view the inevitable conclusion of a conflict between religious opinions and hungry jaws, but for purposes far better adapted to widen and develop the mental energies of the people. This vast amphitheater, with its encircling galleries, its mysterious vaults, and its unseen passages, was an agent of poetic justice, in which crime was punished, or virtue rewarded, by the decrees of an impartial and incorruptible chance.

When a subject was accused of a crime of sufficient importance to interest the king, public notice was given that on an appointed day the fate of the accused person would be decided in the king's arena—a structure which well deserved its name; for, although its form and plan were borrowed from afar, its purpose emanated solely from the brain of this man, who, every barleycorn a king, knew no tradition to which he owed more allegiance than pleased his fancy, and who engrafted on every adopted form of human thought and action the rich growth of his barbaric idealism.

When all the people had assembled in the galleries, and the king, surrounded by his court, sat high up on his throne of royal state on one side of the arena, he gave a signal, a door beneath him opened, and the accused subject stepped out into the amphitheater. Directly opposite him, on the other side of the enclosed space, were two doors, exactly alike and side by

---

rhapsodies: intensely emotional expressions in speech or song
amphitheatre: a round or oval arena for performances, athletic contests, etc.
impartial: fair; not favoring one side or another
engrafted: fastened; attached

side. It was the duty and the privilege of the person on trial to walk directly to these doors and open one of them. He could open either door he pleased. He was subject to no guidance or influence but that of the aforementioned impartial and incorruptible chance. If he opened the one, there came out of it a hungry tiger, the fiercest and most cruel that could be procured, which immediately sprang upon him, and tore him to pieces as a punishment for his guilt. The moment that the case of the criminal was thus decided, doleful iron bells were clanged, great wails went up from the hired mourners posted on the outer rim of the arena, and the vast audience, with bowed heads and downcast hearts, wended slowly their homeward way, mourning greatly that one so young and fair, or so old and respected, should have merited so dire a fate.

But if the accused person opened the other door, there came forth from it a lady, the most suitable to his years and station that his Majesty could select among his fair subjects; and to this lady he was immediately married, as a reward of his innocence. It mattered not that he might already possess a wife and family, or that his affections might be engaged upon an object of his own selection. The king allowed no such subordinate arrangements to interfere with his great scheme of retribution and reward. The exercises, as in the other instance, took place immediately, and in the arena. Another door opened beneath the king, and a priest, followed by a band of choristers, and dancing maidens

procured: obtained
doleful: sad; mournful
wended: proceeded
dire: terrible; having awful consequences
retribution: punishment

blowing joyous airs on golden horns and treading an epithalamic measure, advanced to where the pair stood, side by side, and the wedding was promptly and cheerily solemnized. Then the gay brass bells rang forth their merry peals, the people shouted glad hurrahs, and the innocent man, preceded by children strewing flowers on his path, led his bride to his home.

This was the king's semi-barbaric method of administering justice. Its perfect fairness is obvious. The criminal could not know out of which door would come the lady. He opened either he pleased, without having the slightest idea whether, in the next instant, he was to be devoured or married. On some occasions the tiger came out of one door, and on some out of the other. The decisions of this tribunal were not only fair—they were positively determinate. The accused person was instantly punished if he found himself guilty, and, if innocent he was rewarded on the spot, whether he liked it or not. There was no escape from the judgments of the king's arena.

The institution was a very popular one. When the people gathered together on one of the great trial days, they never knew whether they were to witness a bloody slaughter or a hilarious wedding. This element of uncertainty lent an interest to the occasion which it could not otherwise have attained. Thus the masses were entertained and pleased, and the thinking part of the community could bring no charge of unfairness against this plan; for did not the accused person have the whole matter in his own hands?

----

epithalamic: having to do with marriage (from *epithalamion*, a song or
    poem in praise of a bride or groom)
solemnized: observed or performed with ceremony and ritual
tribunal: a court or committee for administering justice

This semi-barbaric king had a daughter as blooming as his most florid fancies, and with a soul as fervent and imperious as his own. As is usual in such cases, she was the apple of his eye, and was loved by him above all humanity. Among his courtiers was a young man of that fineness of blood and lowness of station common to the conventional heroes of romance who love royal maidens. This royal maiden was well satisfied with her lover, for he was handsome and brave to a degree unsurpassed in all this kingdom, and she loved him with an ardor that had enough of barbarism in it to make it exceedingly warm and strong. This love affair moved on happily for many months, until, one day, the king happened to discover its existence. He did not hesitate nor waver in regard to his duty in the premises. The youth was immediately cast into prison, and a day was appointed for his trial in the king's arena. This, of course, was an especially important occasion, and his Majesty, as well as all the people, was greatly interested in the workings and development of this trial. Never before had such a case occurred—never before had a subject dared to love the daughter of the king. In after years such things became commonplace enough, but then they were in no slight degree novel and startling.

The tiger cages of the kingdom were searched for the most savage and relentless beasts, from which the fiercest monster might be selected for the arena, and the ranks of maiden youth and beauty throughout the land were carefully surveyed by competent judges in order that the young man might have a fitting bride in case fate did not determine for him a different

fervent: highly emotional
imperious: commanding; domineering; overbearing
ardor: a warm, intense emotion
novel: new

destiny. Of course, everybody knew that the deed with which the accused was charged had been done. He had loved the princess, and neither he, she, nor any one else, thought of denying the fact. But the king would not think of allowing any fact of this kind to interfere with the workings of the tribunal, in which he took such great delight and satisfaction. No matter how the affair turned out, the youth would be disposed of, and the king would take an aesthetic pleasure in watching the course of events which would determine whether or not the young man had done wrong in allowing himself to love the princess.

The appointed day arrived. From far and near the people gathered, and thronged the great galleries of the arena, while crowds, unable to gain admittance, massed themselves against its outside walls. The king and his court were in their places, opposite the twin doors—those fateful portals, so terrible in their similarity!

All was ready. The signal was given. A door beneath the royal party opened, and the lover of the princess walked into the arena. Tall, beautiful, fair, his appearance was greeted with a low hum of admiration and anxiety. Half the audience had not known so grand a youth had lived among them. No wonder the princess loved him! What a terrible thing for him to be there!

As the youth advanced into the arena, he turned, as the custom was, to bow to the king. But he did not think at all of that royal personage; his eyes were fixed upon the princess, who sat to the right of her father. Had it not been for the moiety of barbarism in her nature, it is probable that lady

---

aesthetic: artistic
portals: doorways
moiety: half; portion

would not have been there. But her intense and fervid soul would not allow her to be absent on an occasion in which she was so terribly interested. From the moment that the decree had gone forth that her lover should decide his fate in the king's arena, she had thought of nothing, night or day, but this great event and the various subjects connected with it. Possessed of more power, influence, and force of character than any one who had ever before been interested in such a case, she had done what no other person had done—she had possessed herself of the secret of the doors. She knew in which of the two rooms that lay behind those doors stood the cage of the tiger, with its open front, and in which waited the lady. Through these thick doors, heavily curtained with skins on the inside, it was impossible that any noise or suggestion should come from within to the person who should approach to raise the latch of one of them. But gold, and the power of a woman's will, had brought the secret to the princess.

Not only did she know in which room stood the lady ready to emerge, all blushing and radiant, should her door be opened, but she knew who the lady was. It was one of the fairest and loveliest of the damsels of the court who had been selected as the reward of the accused youth, should he be proved innocent of the crime of aspiring to one so far above him; and the princess hated her. Often had she seen, or imagined that she had seen, this fair creature throwing glances of admiration upon the person of her lover, and sometimes she thought these glances were perceived and even returned. Now and then she had seen them talking together. It was but for a moment or two, but much can be

---

fervid: passionate
aspiring: eagerly desiring to achieve or attain something high or great

said in a brief space. It may have been on most unimportant topics, but how could she know that? The girl was lovely, but she had dared to raise her eyes to the loved one of the princess, and, with all the intensity of the savage blood transmitted to her through long lines of wholly barbaric ancestors, she hated the woman who blushed and trembled behind that silent door.

When her lover turned and looked at her, and his eye met hers as she sat there paler and whiter than any one in the vast ocean of anxious faces about her, he saw, by that power of quick perception which is given to those whose souls are one, that she knew behind which door crouched the tiger, and behind which stood the lady. He had expected her to know it. He understood her nature, and his soul was assured that she would never rest until she had made plain to herself this thing, hidden to all other lookers-on, even to the king. The only hope for the youth in which there was any element of certainty was based upon the success of the princess in discovering this mystery, and the moment he looked upon her, he saw she had succeeded, as in his soul he knew she had succeeded.

Then it was that his quick and anxious glance asked the question, "Which?" It was as plain to her as if he shouted it from where he stood. There was not an instant to be lost. The question was asked in a flash; it must be answered in another.

Her right arm lay on the cushioned parapet before her. She raised her hand, and made a slight, quick movement toward the right. No one but her lover saw her. Every eye but his was fixed on the man in the arena.

He turned, and with a firm and rapid step he walked across the empty space. Every heart stopped beating, every

---

parapet: a low wall or railing around a platform

breath was held, every eye was fixed immovably upon that man. Without the slightest hesitation, he went to the door on the right, and opened it.

Now, the point of the story is this: Did the tiger come out of that door, or did the lady?

The more we reflect upon this question, the harder it is to answer. It involves a study of the human heart which leads us through devious mazes of passion, out of which it is difficult to find our way. Think of it, fair reader, not as if the decision of the question depended upon yourself, but upon that hot-blooded, semi-barbaric princess, her soul at a white heat beneath the combined fires of despair and jealousy. She had lost him, but who should have him?

How often, in her waking hours and in her dreams, had she started in wild horror, and covered her face with her hands as she thought of her lover opening the door on the other side of which waited the cruel fangs of the tiger!

But how much oftener had she seen him at the other door! How in her grievous reveries had she gnashed her teeth and torn her hair when she saw his start of rapturous delight as he opened the door of the lady! How her soul had burned in agony when she had seen him rush to meet that woman, with her flushing cheek and sparkling eye of triumph; when she had seen him lead her forth, his whole frame kindled with the joy of recovered life; when she had heard the glad shouts from the multitude, and the wild ringing of the happy bells; when she had seen the priest, with his joyous followers, advance to

_____

devious: roundabout; wandering; misleading
grievous: characterized by pain and extreme suffering
reveries: daydreams

the couple, and make them man and wife before her very eyes; and when she had seen them walk away together upon their path of flowers, followed by the tremendous shouts of the hilarious multitude, in which her one despairing shriek was lost and drowned!

Would it not be better for him to die at once, and go to wait for her in the blessed regions of semi-barbaric futurity?

And yet, that awful tiger, those shrieks, that blood!

Her decision had been indicated in an instant, but it had been made after days and nights of anguished deliberation. She had known she would be asked, she had decided what she would answer, and, without the slightest hesitation, she had moved her hand to the right.

The question of her decision is one not to be lightly considered, and it is not for me to presume to set myself up as the one person able to answer it. So I leave it with all of you: Which came out of the opened door—the lady, or the tiger?

TO EVERYTHING THERE IS A SEASON

SPRING AND FALL
TO A YOUNG CHILD
by Gerard Manley Hopkins

Márgarét, áre you gríeving
Over Goldengrove unleaving?
Leáves, líke the things of man, you
With your fresh thoughts care for, can you?
Áh! ás the heart grows older
It will come to such sights colder
By and by, nor spare a sigh
Though worlds of wanwood leafmeal lie;
And yet you *will* weep and know why.
Now no matter, child, the name:
Sórrow's spríngs áre the same.
Nor mouth had, no nor mind, expressed
What heart heard of, ghost guessed:
It ís the blight man was born for,
It is Margaret you mourn for.

---

unleaving: losing leaves
wanwood: *probably* wan (pale, sickly, feeble) + wood (forest)
leafmeal: *probably* leaf + piecemeal (in pieces), thus, with leaves fallen
   in pieces
ghost: spirit; soul
blight: a disease that injures or kills plants; something that crushes one's
   hopes or plans; something that harms or destroys

IN JUST

by e.e. cummings

in Just–
spring   when the world is mud-
luscious the little
lame balloonman

whistles   far   and wee

and eddieandbill come
running from marbles and
piracies and it's
spring

when the world is puddle-wonderful

the queer
old balloonman whistles
far   and   wee
and bettyandisbel come dancing

from hop-scotch and jump-rope and

---

luscious: delicious; appealing strongly to the senses

it's
spring
and
    the

       goat-footed

balloonMan   whistles
far
and
wee

July

by Susan Hartley Swett

When the scarlet cardinal tells
    Her dream to the dragonfly,
And the lazy breeze makes a nest in the trees,
    And murmurs a lullaby,
        It is July.

When the tangled cobweb pulls
    The cornflower's cap awry,
And the lilies tall lean over the wall
    To bow to the butterfly,
        It is July.

When the heat like a mist veil floats,
    And poppies flame in the rye,
And the silver note in the streamlet's throat
    Has softened almost to a sigh,
        It is July.

When the hours are so still that time
    Forgets them, and lets them lie
'Neath petals pink till the night stars wink
    At the sunset in the sky,
        It is July.

---

awry: out of place; askew
streamlet: a small stream

When each fingerpost by the way
Says that Slumbertown is nigh;
When the grass is tall, and the roses fall,
And nobody wonders why,
It is July.

fingerpost: a guidepost with a sign shaped like a pointing finger
nigh: near

To Autumn
by John Keats

1

Season of mists and mellow fruitfulness,
    Close bosom-friend of the maturing sun;
Conspiring with him how to load and bless
    With fruit the vines that round the thatch-eves run;
To bend with apples the moss'd cottage-trees,
    And fill all fruit with ripeness to the core;
      To swell the gourd, and plump the hazel shells
    With a sweet kernel; to set budding more,
And still more, later flowers for the bees,
Until they think warm days will never cease,
      For summer has o'er-brimm'd their clammy cells.

2

Who hath not seen thee oft amid thy store?
    Sometimes whoever seeks abroad may find
Thee sitting careless on a granary floor,
    Thy hair soft-lifted by the winnowing wind;

---

bosom-friend: a dear, cherished friend
conspiring: planning or plotting together
thatch-eves: the overhanging edges (*eaves*) of a roof covered with straw,
    reeds, or similar material (*thatch*)
o'erbrimm'd: filled to overflowing
oft: often
amid: surrounded by; in the middle of
store: abundance; a great quantity
granary: a building where grain is stored
winnowing: from *winnow* = to blow away the chaff (seed coverings) from
    the grain

Or on a half-reap'd furrow sound asleep,
   Drows'd with the fume of poppies, while thy hook
   Spares the next swath and all its twined flowers:
And sometimes like a gleaner thou dost keep
   Steady thy laden head across a brook;
   Or by a cyder-press, with patient look,
Thou watchest the last oozings hours by hours.

3

Where are the songs of spring? Ay, where are they?
   Think not of them, thou hast thy music too,—
While barred clouds bloom the soft-dying day,
   And touch the stubble-plains with rosy hue;
Then in a wailful choir the small gnats mourn
   Among the river sallows, borne aloft
   Or sinking as the light wind lives or dies;
And full-grown lambs loud bleat from hilly bourn;
   Hedge-crickets sing; and now with treble soft
   The red-breast whistles from a garden-croft;
   And gathering swallows twitter in the skies.

---

furrow: a groove cut in a field by a plow
drows'd: made sleepy
fume: vapor
hook: a scythe (a long curved blade at the end of a handle, used for
   cutting grain)
swath: a row or strip; the path cut by a scythe
gleaner: one who gathers grain left behind by reapers
laden: carrying a burden
stubble-plains: fields covered by short stalks of grain left behind after harvesting
sallows: willow trees
bourn: region (from an old meaning of bourn as "boundary")
croft: a small field enclosed by a fence or wall

IT SIFTS FROM LEADEN SIEVES
by Emily Dickinson

It sifts from Leaden Sieves —
It powders all the Wood.
It fills with Alabaster Wool
The Wrinkles of the Road —

It makes an Even Face
Of Mountain, and of Plain —
Unbroken Forehead from the East
Unto the East again —

It reaches to the Fence —
It wraps it Rail by Rail
Till it is lost in Fleeces —
It deals Celestial Vail

To Stump, and Stack — and Stem —
A Summer's empty Room —
Acres of Joints, where Harvests were,
Recordless, but for them —

---

leaden: like lead; dull and heavy; dark gray in color
alabaster: a kind of fine white stone often carved into vases or ornaments
celestial: relating to the sky or the heavens

It Ruffles Wrists of Posts
As Ankles of a Queen —
Then stills its Artisans — like Ghosts —
Denying they have been —

artisans: skilled craftsmen

THE SNOW-STORM
by Ralph Waldo Emerson

Announced by all the trumpets of the sky,
Arrives the snow, and, driving o'er the fields,
Seems nowhere to alight: the whited air
Hides hills and woods, the river, and the heaven,
And veils the farm-house at the garden's end.
The sled and traveler stopped, the courier's feet
Delayed, all friends shut out, the housemates sit
Around the radiant fireplace, enclosed
In a tumultuous privacy of storm.

Come see the north wind's masonry.
Out of an unseen quarry evermore
Furnished with tile, the fierce artificer
Curves his white bastions with projected roof
Round every windward stake, or tree, or door.
Speeding, the myriad-handed, his wild work
So fanciful, so savage, nought cares he

---

alight: to land; to come to rest
courier: a messenger
tumultuous: noisy and confused; disorderly
masonry: stone or brickwork
quarry: a pit from which stone is cut or dug
evermore: always
artificer: a skilled craftsman; an artist
bastions: protective walls that project outward
windward: facing the direction from which the wind is blowing
myriad: a great many; a vast number
nought (also spelled *naught*): nothing

For number or proportion. Mockingly,
On coop or kennel he hangs Parian wreaths;
A swan-like form invests the hidden thorn;
Fills up the farmer's lane from wall to wall,
Maugre the farmer sighs; and at the gate,
A tapering turret overtops the work.
And when his hours are numbered, and the world
Is all his own, retiring, as he were not,
Leaves, when the sun appears, astonished Art
To mimic in slow structures, stone by stone,
Built in an age, the mad wind's night-work,
The frolic architecture of the snow.

Parian: looking like white marble (from Páros, the Greek island known
    for its fine marble)
invests: adorns; covers
maugre: in spite of; regardless of
tapering: becoming thinner or narrower at one end
turret: a small tower or tower-like structure
mimic: to copy; to imitate
frolic: playful; merry

MAKING US SEE

A Night Ride in a Prairie Schooner

by Hamlin Garland

The following selection is the first chapter of Boy Life on the Prairie, *a book published by the American writer Hamlin Garland in 1899. "It was my intention," said Garland, "to delineate the work and plans of a boy on a prairie farm from season to season." This boy, Lincoln Stewart, was in many ways the young Hamlin Garland himself, who grew up on the Iowa prairie in the years just after the Civil War.* Boy Life on the Prairie *blends autobiography and fiction. As Garland explained, "All of the events, even those in fictional form, are actual, although in some cases I have combined experiences of other boys with my own."*

One afternoon in the autumn of 1868 Duncan Stewart, leading his little fleet of "prairie schooners," entered upon "The Big Prairie" of northern Iowa, and pushed resolutely on into the west. His four-horse canvas-covered wagon was followed by two other lighter vehicles, one of which was driven by his wife, and the other by a hired freighter. At the rear of all the wagons, and urging forward a dozen or sixteen cattle, trotted a gaunt youth and a small boy.

---

prairie schooner: a covered wagon, that is, a wagon with an arched canvas
    cover, pulled by horses or oxen, used by American pioneers in the
    nineteenth century (a *schooner* is a sailing ship)
resolutely: with great determination
freighter: one who transports things from one place to another
gaunt: extremely thin

The boy had tears upon his face, and was limping with a stone-bruise. He could hardly look over the wild oats, which tossed their gleaming bayonets in the wind, and when he dashed out into the blue joint and wild sunflowers, to bring the cattle into the road, he could be traced only by the ripple he made, like a trout in a pool. He was a small edition of his father. He wore the same color and check in his hickory shirt and his long pantaloons of blue denim had suspenders precisely like those of the men. Indeed, he considered himself a man, notwithstanding the tear-stains on his brown cheeks.

It seemed a long time since leaving his native Wisconsin coulee behind, with only a momentary sadness, but now, after nearly a week of travel, it seemed his father must be leading them all to the edge of the world, and Lincoln was very sad and weary.

"Company, halt!" called the Captain.

One by one the teams stopped, and the cattle began to feed (they were always ready to eat), and Mr. Stewart, coming back where his wife sat, said cheerily:

"Well, Kate, here's the big prairie I told you of, and beyond that blue line of timber you see is Sun Prairie, and home."

Mrs. Stewart did not smile. She was too weary, and the wailing of little Mary in her arms was dispiriting.

---

bayonets: blades attached to the ends of rifles (here used figuratively to describe wild oats)
blue joint: a kind of tall-growing grass
pantaloons: pants
coulee: in Midwest usage, *coulee* refers to a valley with hills on either side
dispiriting: discouraging

"Come here, Lincoln," said Mr. Stewart. "Here we are, out of sight of the works of man. Not a house in sight—climb up here and see."

Lincoln rustled along through the tall grass, and, clambering up the wagon wheel, stood silently beside his mother. Tired as he was, the scene made an indelible impression on him. It was as though he had suddenly been transported into another world, a world where time did not exist; where snow never fell, and the grass waved forever under a cloudless sky. A great awe fell upon him as he looked, and he could not utter a word.

At last Mr. Stewart cheerily called: "Attention, battalion! We must reach Sun Prairie tonight. *Forward, march!*"

Again the little wagon train took up its slow way through the tall ranks of the wild oats, and the drooping, flaming sunflowers. Slowly the sun sank. The crickets began to cry, the nighthawks whizzed and boomed, and long before the prairie was crossed the night had come.

Being too tired to foot it any longer behind the cracking heels of the cows, Lincoln climbed into the wagon beside his little brother, who was already asleep, and, resting his head against his mother's knee, lay for a long time, listening to the *chuck-chuckle* of the wheels, watching the light go out of the sky, and counting the stars as they appeared.

At last they entered the wood, which seemed a very threatening place indeed, and his alert ears caught every sound,—the hoot of owls, the quavering cry of coons, the twitter of night birds. But at last his weariness overcame him, and he dozed off, hearing the clank of the whippletrees, the creak of the horses' harness, the vibrant voice of his father,

---

indelible: not able to be erased or forgotten
whippletrees (also *whiffletrees*): movable bars that link an animal's harness
    to the vehicle the animal pulls

and the occasional cry of the hired hand, urging the cattle forward through the dark.

He was roused once by the ripple of a stream, wherein the horses thrust their hot nozzles, he heard the grind of wheels on the pebbly bottom, and the wild shouts of the resolute men as they scrambled up the opposite bank, and entered once more the dark aisles of the forest. Here the road was smoother, and to the soft rumble of the wheels the boy slept.

At last, deep in the night, so it seemed to Lincoln, his father shouted: "Wake up, everybody. We're almost home." Then, facing the darkness, he cried, in western fashion, "Hello! the house!"

Dazed and stupid, Lincoln stepped down the wheel to the ground, his legs numb with sleep. Owen followed, querulous as a sick puppy, and together they stood in the darkness, waiting further command.

From a small frame house, near by, a man with a lantern appeared.

"Hello!" he said, yawning with sleep. "Is that you, Stewart? I'd jest about give you up."

While the men unhitched the teams, Stewart helped his wife and children to the house, where Mrs. Hutchinson, a tall, thin woman with a pleasant smile, made them welcome. She helped Mrs. Stewart remove her things, and then set out some bread and milk for the boys, which they ate in silence, their heavy eyelids drooping.

When Mr. Stewart came in, he said: "Now, Lincoln, you and Will are to sleep in the other shack. Run right along, before you go to sleep. Owen will stay here."

---

nozzles: noses; snouts
querulous: whiny; continually complaining

Without in the least knowing the why or wherefore, Lincoln set forth beside the hired man, out into the unknown. They walked rapidly for a long time, and, as his blood began to stir again, Lincoln awoke to the wonder and mystery of the hour. The strange grasses under his feet, the unknown stars over his head, the dim objects on the horizon, were all the fashioning of a mind in the world of dreams. His soul ached with the passion of his remembered visions and his forebodings.

At last they came to a small cabin on the banks of a deep ravine. Opening the door, the men lit a candle, and spread their burden of blankets on the floor. Lincoln crept between them like a sleepy puppy, and in a few minutes this unknown actual world merged itself in the mystery of dreams.

When he woke, the sun was shining, hot and red, through the open windows, and the men were smoking their pipes by the rough fence before the door. Lincoln hurried out to see what kind of a world this was to which his night's journey had hurried him. It was, for the most part, a level land, covered with short grass intermixed with tall weeds, and with many purple and yellow flowers. A little way off, to the right, stood a small house, and about as far to the right was another, before which stood the wagons belonging to his father. Directly in front was a wide expanse of rolling prairie, cut by a deep ravine, while to the north, beyond the small farm which was fenced, a still wider region rolled away into unexplored and marvelous distance. Altogether it was a land to exalt a boy who had lived all his life in a thickly settled Wisconsin coulee, where the horizon line was high and small of circuit.

------

forebodings: anxious expectations
exalt: to fill with intense emotion

In less than two hours the wagons were unloaded, the stove was set up in the kitchen, the family clock was ticking on its shelf, and the bureau set against the wall. It was amazing to see how these familiar things and his mother's bustling presence changed the looks of the cabin. Little Mary was quite happy crawling about the floor, and Owen, who had explored the barn and found a lizard to play with, was entirely at home. Lincoln had climbed to the roof of the house, and was still trying to comprehend this mighty stretch of grasses. Sitting astride the roof board, he gazed away into the northwest, where no house broke the horizon line, wondering what lay beyond that high ridge.

While seated thus, he heard a distant roar and trample, and saw a cloud of dust rising along the fence which bounded the farm to the west. It was like the rush of a whirlwind, and, before he could call to his father, out on the smooth sod to the south burst a platoon of wild horses, led by a beautiful roan mare. The boy's heart leaped with excitement as the shaggy colts swept round to the east, racing like wolves at play. Their long tails and abundant manes streamed in the wind like banners, and their imperious bugling voiced their contempt for man.

Lincoln clapped his hands with joy, and all of the family ran to the fence to enjoy the sight. A boy, splendidly mounted on a fleet roan, the mate of the leader, was riding at a slashing pace, with intent to turn the troop to the south. He was a superb rider, and the little Morgan strove gallantly without

---

roan: having a red or brown coat with white or gray thickly mixed in; or,
    a horse with this coloring
imperious: regally commanding; domineering
contempt: disdain; scorn

need of whip or spur. He laid out like a hare. He seemed to float like a hawk, skimming the weeds, and her rider sat him like one born to the saddle, erect and supple, and of little hindrance to the beast.

On swept the herd, circling to the left, heading for the wild lands to the east. Gallantly strove the roan with his resolute rider, disdaining to be beaten by his own mate, his breath roaring like a furnace, his nostrils blown like trumpets, his hoofs pounding the resounding sod.

All in vain; even with the inside track he was no match for his wild, free mate. The herd drew ahead, and, plunging through a short lane, vanished over a big swell to the east, and their drumming rush died rapidly away into silence.

This was a glorious introduction to the life of the prairies, and Lincoln's heart filled with boundless joy, and longing to know it—all of it, east, west, north, and south. He had no further wish to return to his coulee home. The horseman had become his ideal, the prairie his domain.

---

supple: flexible; bending easily
hindrance: an impediment; an obstacle; something that holds back or gets in the way
resounding: filled with sound; echoing

WALDEN POND
by Henry David Thoreau

"I went to the woods," said Henry David Thoreau, "because I wished to live deliberately." The woods he went to were on the shores of Walden Pond, near Concord, Massachusetts. For two years he lived alone in a cabin, only rarely receiving visitors or going to town. He spent his time observing the workings of nature, thinking, and writing. In 1854 he published Walden, or Life in the Woods. *The book, an American classic, celebrates the natural world as well as the ability of the individual to live free from the pressures and restrictions of society. In the following excerpt from* Walden, *Thoreau describes and muses upon the pond that gave his book its title.*

Standing on the smooth sandy beach at the east end of the pond, in a calm September afternoon, when a slight haze makes the opposite shore-line indistinct, I have seen whence came the expression, "the glassy surface of a lake." When you invert your head, it looks like a thread of finest gossamer stretched across the valley, and gleaming against the distant pine woods, separating one stratum of the atmosphere from another. You would think that you could walk dry under it to the opposite hills, and that the swallows which skim over might perch on it. Indeed, they sometimes dive below this line, as it were by mistake, and are undeceived.

---

whence: from where; from which
invert: to turn upside down or inside out
gossamer: a thin, delicate fabric
stratum: a level or layer

As you look over the pond westward you are obliged to employ both your hands to defend your eyes against the reflected as well as the true sun, for they are equally bright; and if, between the two, you survey its surface critically, it is literally as smooth as glass, except where the skater insects, at equal intervals scattered over its whole extent, by their motions in the sun produce the finest imaginable sparkle on it, or, perchance, a duck plumes itself, or, as I have said, a swallow skims so low as to touch it. It may be that in the distance a fish describes an arc of three or four feet in the air, and there is one bright flash where it emerges, and another where it strikes the water; sometimes the whole silvery arc is revealed; or here and there, perhaps, is a thistle-down floating on its surface, which the fishes dart at and so dimple it again. It is like molten glass cooled but not congealed, and the few motes in it are pure and beautiful like the imperfections in glass.

You may often detect a yet smoother and darker water, separated from the rest as if by an invisible cobweb, boom of the water nymphs, resting on it. From a hilltop you can see a fish leap in almost any part; for not a pickerel or shiner picks an insect from this smooth surface but it manifestly disturbs the equilibrium of the whole lake. It is wonderful with what

---

obliged: required
skater: a long-legged insect that skims over the surface of water
perchance: perhaps; possibly
thistle-down: the soft, feathery hairs attached to the fruit of a thistle plant
molten: made into liquid by intense heat
congealed: solidified
motes: specks; small particles
boom: a floating barrier
pickerel, shiner: types of freshwater fish
manifestly: obviously; easily perceived or understood
equilibrium: a state of balance

elaborateness this simple fact is advertised,—this piscine murder will out,—and from my distant perch I distinguish the circling undulations when they are half a dozen rods in diameter. You can even detect a water-bug (*Gyrinus*) ceaselessly progressing over the smooth surface a quarter of a mile off; for they furrow the water slightly, making a conspicuous ripple bounded by two diverging lines, but the skaters glide over it without rippling it perceptibly. When the surface is considerably agitated there are no skaters nor water-bugs on it, but apparently, in calm days, they leave their havens and adventurously glide forth from the shore by short impulses till they completely cover it.

It is a soothing employment, on one of those fine days in the fall when all the warmth of the sun is fully appreciated, to sit on a stump on such a height as this, overlooking the pond, and study the dimpling circles which are incessantly inscribed on its otherwise invisible surface amid the reflected skies and trees. Over this great expanse there is no disturbance but it is thus at once gently smoothed away and assuaged, as, when a vase of water is jarred, the trembling circles seek the shore

---

piscine: relating to fish
murder will out: an expression meaning that a crime cannot be hidden, but will be discovered and punished
undulations: wavelike movements
rods: measures of distance, with one rod = 16.5 feet
furrow: to make grooves or wrinkles in
conspicuous: obvious; standing out; attracting attention
diverging: moving in different directions from a common starting point
perceptibly: noticeably
agitated: disturbed; moved
havens: safe places
incessantly: constantly; unceasingly
inscribed: written on; carved in
assuaged: soothed

and all is smooth again. Not a fish can leap or an insect fall on the pond but it is thus reported in circling dimples, in lines of beauty, as it were the constant welling up of its fountain, the gentle pulsing of its life, the heaving of its breast. The thrills of joy and thrills of pain are undistinguishable. How peaceful the phenomena of the lake! Again the works of man shine as in the spring. Ay, every leaf and twig and stone and cobweb sparkles now at mid-afternoon as when covered with dew in a spring morning. Every motion of an oar or an insect produces a flash of light; and if an oar falls, how sweet the echo!

In such a day, in September or October, Walden is a perfect forest mirror, set round with stones as precious to my eye as if fewer or rarer. Nothing so fair, so pure, and at the same time so large, as a lake, perchance, lies on the surface of the earth. Sky water. It needs no fence. Nations come and go without defiling it. It is a mirror which no stone can crack, whose quicksilver will never wear off, whose gilding Nature continually repairs; no storms, no dust, can dim its surface ever fresh;—a mirror in which all impurity presented to it sinks, swept and dusted by the sun's hazy brush,—this the light dust-cloth,—which retains no breath that is breathed on it, but sends its own to float as clouds high above its surface, and be reflected in its bosom still....

One November afternoon, in the calm at the end of a rain storm of several days' duration, when the sky was still completely overcast and the air was full of mist, I observed that the pond was remarkably smooth, so that it was difficult

---

phenomena: observable events
defiling: polluting; making unclean or impure
quicksilver: mercury, once used in the manufacture of mirrors
gilding: a thin coating of gold

to distinguish its surface; though it no longer reflected the bright tints of October, but the somber November colors of the surrounding hills. Though I passed over it as gently as possible, the slight undulations produced by my boat extended almost as far as I could see, and gave a ribbed appearance to the reflections.

But, as I was looking over the surface, I saw here and there at a distance a faint glimmer, as if some skater insects which had escaped the frosts might be collected there, or, perchance, the surface, being so smooth, betrayed where a spring welled up from the bottom. Paddling gently to one of these places, I was surprised to find myself surrounded by myriads of small perch, about five inches long, of a rich bronze color in the green water, sporting there and constantly rising to the surface and dimpling it, sometimes leaving bubbles on it. In such transparent and seemingly bottomless water, reflecting the clouds, I seemed to be floating through the air as in a balloon, and their swimming impressed me as a kind of flight or hovering, as if they were a compact flock of birds passing just beneath my level on the right or left, their fins, like sails, set all around them....

An old man who used to frequent this pond nearly sixty years ago, when it was dark with surrounding forests, tells me that in those days he sometimes saw it all alive with ducks and other water fowl, and that there were many eagles about it. He came here a-fishing, and used an old log canoe which he found on the shore. It was made of two white pine logs dug out and pinned together, and was cut off square at the ends. It was very clumsy, but lasted a great many years

---

perch: a type of freshwater fish

before it became waterlogged and perhaps sank to the bottom. He did not know whose it was; it belonged to the pond. He used to make a cable for his anchor of strips of hickory bark tied together. An old man, a potter, who lived by the pond before the Revolution, told him once that there was an iron chest at the bottom, and that he had seen it. Sometimes it would come floating up to the shore; but when you went toward it, it would go back into deep water and disappear. I was pleased to hear of the old log canoe, which took the place of an Indian one of the same material but more graceful construction, which perchance had first been a tree on the bank, and then, as it were, fell into the water, to float there for a generation, the most proper vessel for the lake. I remember that when I first looked into these depths there were many large trunks to be seen indistinctly lying on the bottom, which had either been blown over formerly, or left on the ice at the last cutting, when wood was cheaper; but now they have mostly disappeared.

When I first paddled a boat on Walden, it was completely surrounded by thick and lofty pine and oak woods, and in some of its coves grape vines had run over the trees next the water and formed bowers under which a boat could pass. The hills which form its shores are so steep, and the woods on them were then so high, that, as you looked down from the west end, it had the appearance of an amphitheatre for some kind of sylvan spectacle. I have spent many an hour, when I was younger, floating over its surface as the zephyr

---

amphitheatre: a round or oval arena for performances, athletic contests, etc.
sylvan: having to do with woods and forests
spectacle: a public performance or display
zephyr: a gentle breeze

willed, having paddled my boat to the middle, and lying on my back across the seats, in a summer forenoon, dreaming awake, until I was aroused by the boat touching the sand, and I arose to see what shore my fates had impelled me to; days when idleness was the most attractive and productive industry. Many a forenoon have I stolen away, preferring to spend thus the most valued part of the day; for I was rich, if not in money, in sunny hours and summer days, and spent them lavishly; nor do I regret that I did not waste more of them in the workshop or the teacher's desk. But since I left those shores the woodchoppers have still further laid them waste, and now for many a year there will be no more rambling through the aisles of the wood, with occasional vistas through which you see the water. My Muse may be excused if she is silent henceforth. How can you expect the birds to sing when their groves are cut down?

---

forenoon: morning
impelled: driven forward
lavishly: extravagantly; very generously
vistas: views
Muse: an inspirational force; in Greek mythology, any of the nine
    goddesses that inspired creativity in mortals
henceforth: from now on

from

PILGRIM AT TINKER CREEK
by Annie Dillard

Annie Dillard was born in 1945 in Pittsburgh, Pennsylvania. She began writing poetry in high school. In college, she wrote a long essay on Thoreau's Walden. *Like Thoreau, Dillard is a close observer of the natural world, and a deep thinker about the meanings of all she observes.*

After a severe illness in 1971, Dillard lived for a year by Tinker Creek in the Blue Ridge Mountains of Virginia. Surrounded by the woods, she walked, watched, and pondered. She recorded her thoughts and observations in a journal that became the basis for a book, Pilgrim at Tinker Creek. *The book was awarded the Pulitzer Prize for nonfiction in 1975.*

"In nature," Dillard has said, "I find grace tangled in a rapture with violence; …I find mystery, newness, and a kind of exuberant, spendthrift energy." The following excerpt from Pilgrim at Tinker Creek *gives a sense of how Dillard perceives the natural world—with clarity and awe.*

A couple of summers ago I was walking along the edge of the island to see what I could see in the water, and mainly to scare frogs. Frogs have an inelegant way of taking off from invisible positions on the bank just ahead of your feet, in dire panic, emitting a froggy, "Yike!" and splashing into the water. Incredibly, this amused me, and, incredibly, it amuses me still.

---

inelegant: graceless; lacking refinement
dire: desperate; terrible

As I walked along the grassy edge of the island, I got better and better at seeing frogs both in and out of the water. I learned to recognize, slowing down, the difference in texture of the light reflected from mudbank, water, grass, or frog. Frogs were flying all around me. At the end of the island I noticed a small green frog. He was exactly half in and half out of water, looking like a schematic diagram of an amphibian, and he didn't jump.

He didn't jump; I crept closer. At last I knelt on the island's winterkilled grass, lost, dumbstruck, staring at the frog in the creek just four feet away. He was a very small frog with wide, dull eyes. And just as I looked at him, he slowly crumpled and began to sag. The spirit vanished from his eyes as if snuffed. His skin emptied and dropped; his very skull seemed to collapse and settle like a kicked tent. He was shrinking before my eyes like a deflating football. I watched the taut, glistening skin on his shoulders ruck, and rumple, and fall. Soon, part of his skin, formless as a pricked balloon, lay in floating folds like bright scum on top of the water; it was a monstrous and terrifying thing. I gaped bewildered, appalled. An oval shadow hung in the water behind the drained frog; then the shadow glided away. The frog skin bag started to sink.

I had read about the giant water bug, but never seen one. "Giant water bug" is really the name of the creature, which is an enormous, heavy-bodied brown beetle. It eats insects, tadpoles, fish, and frogs. Its grasping forelegs are mighty

---

snuffed: put out (as one might snuff a candle)
taut: pulled tight
ruck: to become creased or wrinkled
gaped: stared with one's mouth open
appalled: filled with fear, dread, dismay

and hooked inward. It seizes a victim with these legs, hugs it tight, and paralyzes it with enzymes injected during a vicious bite. That one bite is the only bite it ever takes. Through the puncture shoot the poisons that dissolve the victim's muscles and bones and organs—all but the skin—and through it the giant water bug sucks out the victim's body reduced to a juice. This event is quite common in warm fresh water. The frog I saw was being sucked by a giant water bug. I had been kneeling on the island grass; when the unrecognizable flap of frog skin settled on the creek bottom, swaying, I stood up and brushed the knees of my pants. I couldn't catch my breath....

About five years ago I saw a mockingbird make a straight vertical descent from the roof-gutter of a four-story building. It was an act as careless and spontaneous as the curl of a stem or the kindling of a star.

The mockingbird took a single step into the air and dropped. His wings were still folded against his sides as though he were singing from a limb and not falling, accelerating thirty-two feet per second per second, through empty air. Just a breath before he would have been dashed to the ground, he unfurled his wings with exact, deliberate care, revealing the broad bars of white, spread his elegant, white-banded tail, and so floated onto the grass. I had just rounded a corner when his insouciant step caught my eye; there was no one else in sight. The fact

---

enzymes: any of various proteins produced by living organisms
descent: a downward movement
kindling: catching fire; bursting into flame
thirty-two feet per second per second: the rate at which a falling body
    accelerates toward the ground
insouciant: casual; nonchalant; without concern

of his free fall was like the old philosophical conundrum about the tree that falls in the forest. The answer must be, I think, that beauty and grace are performed whether or not we will or sense them. The least we can do is try to be there.

Another time I saw another wonder: sharks off the Atlantic coast of Florida. There is a way a wave rises above the ocean horizon, a triangular wedge against the sky. If you stand where the ocean breaks on a shallow beach, you see the raised water in a wave is translucent, shot with lights. One late afternoon at low tide a hundred big sharks passed the beach near the mouth of the tidal river in a feeding frenzy. As each green wave rose from the churning water, it illuminated within itself the six- or eight-foot-long bodies of twisting sharks. The sharks disappeared as each wave rolled toward me; then a new wave would swell above the horizon, containing in it, like scorpions in amber, sharks that roiled and heaved. The sight held awesome wonders: power and beauty, grace tangled in a rapture with violence.

---

conundrum: a riddle; a difficult question or problem
translucent: allowing light to pass through
amber: a hard yellowish-orange fossilized resin (in which insects are sometimes trapped and preserved)
roiled: moved violently
rapture: a state of extreme emotion; ecstasy

VOICES AND VIEWPOINTS

THE RAINY DAY
by Henry Wadsworth Longfellow

The day is cold, and dark, and dreary;
It rains, and the wind is never weary;
The vine still clings to the moldering wall,
But at every gust the dead leaves fall,
 And the day is dark and dreary.

My life is cold, and dark, and dreary;
It rains, and the wind is never weary;
My thoughts still cling to the moldering Past,
But the hopes of youth fall thick in the blast,
 And the days are dark and dreary.

Be still, sad heart! and cease repining;
Behind the clouds is the sun still shining;
Thy fate is the common fate of all,
Into each life some rain must fall,
 Some days must be dark and dreary.

---

moldering: crumbling; falling apart
blast: a strong gust of wind
repining: feeling downcast and discontent; fretting

INVICTUS

by William Ernest Henley

Out of the night that covers me,
　Black as the Pit from pole to pole,
I thank whatever gods may be
　For my unconquerable soul.

In the fell clutch of circumstance
　I have not winced nor cried aloud.
Under the bludgeonings of chance
　My head is bloody, but unbowed.

Beyond this place of wrath and tears
　Looms but the Horror of the shade,
And yet the menace of the years
　Finds, and shall find, me unafraid.

It matters not how strait the gate,
　How charged with punishments the scroll,
I am the master of my fate;
　I am the captain of my soul.

---

the Pit: hell
fell: cruel; sinister; fierce
bludgeonings: brutal beatings, as with a heavy club
shade: the realm of the dead
menace: threat
strait: narrow

WE REAL COOL

by Gwendolyn Brooks

The Pool Players.
Seven at the Golden Shovel.

We real cool. We
Left school. We

Lurk late. We
Strike straight. We

Sing sin. We
Thin gin. We

Jazz June. We
Die soon.

THE NEGRO SPEAKS OF RIVERS

by Langston Hughes

I've known rivers:
I've known rivers ancient as the world and older than the
    flow of human blood in human veins.

My soul has grown deep like the rivers.

I bathed in the Euphrates when dawns were young.
I built my hut near the Congo and it lulled me to sleep.
I looked upon the Nile and raised the pyramids above it.
I heard the singing of the Mississippi when Abe Lincoln
    went down to New Orleans, and I've seen its muddy
    bosom turn all golden in the sunset.

I've known rivers:
Ancient, dusky rivers.

My soul has grown deep like the rivers.

MENDING WALL

by Robert Frost

Something there is that doesn't love a wall,
That sends the frozen-ground-swell under it,
And spills the upper boulders in the sun,
And makes gaps even two can pass abreast.
The work of hunters is another thing:
I have come after them and made repair
Where they have left not one stone on a stone,
But they would have the rabbit out of hiding,
To please the yelping dogs. The gaps I mean,
No one has seen them made or heard them made,
But at spring mending-time we find them there.
I let my neighbor know beyond the hill;
And on a day we meet to walk the line
And set the wall between us once again.
We keep the wall between us as we go.
To each the boulders that have fallen to each.
And some are loaves and some so nearly balls
We have to use a spell to make them balance:
"Stay where you are until our backs are turned!"
We wear our fingers rough with handling them.
Oh, just another kind of outdoor game,

---

mending: fixing; repairing
abreast: side by side

One on a side. It comes to little more:
There where it is we do not need the wall:
He is all pine and I am apple orchard.
My apple trees will never get across
And eat the cones under his pines, I tell him.
He only says, "Good fences make good neighbors."
Spring is the mischief in me, and I wonder
If I could put a notion in his head:
"*Why* do they make good neighbors? Isn't it
Where there are cows? But here there are no cows.
Before I built a wall I'd ask to know
What I was walling in or walling out,
And to whom I was like to give offence.
Something there is that doesn't love a wall,
That wants it down." I could say "Elves" to him,
But it's not elves exactly, and I'd rather
He said it for himself. I see him there
Bringing a stone grasped firmly by the top
In each hand, like an old-stone savage armed.
He moves in darkness as it seems to me,
Not of woods only and the shade of trees.
He will not go behind his father's saying,
And he likes having thought of it so well
He says again, "Good fences make good neighbors."

TWO SONNETS
by William Shakespeare

18

Shall I compare thee to a summer's day?
Thou art more lovely and more temperate.
Rough winds do shake the darling buds of May,
And summer's lease hath all too short a date.
Sometime too hot the eye of heaven shines,
And often is his gold complexion dimmed,
And every fair from fair sometime declines,
By chance or nature's changing course untrimmed;
But thy eternal summer shall not fade
Nor lose possession of that fair thou ow'st,
Nor shall death brag thou wander'st in his shade
When in eternal lines to time thou grow'st:
    So long as men can breathe or eyes can see,
    So long lives this, and this gives life to thee.

---

temperate: mild
lease: term of existence
fair: beauty
untrimmed: stripped of adornments
ow'st: ownest (own)

29

When, in disgrace with fortune and men's eyes,
I all alone beweep my outcast state,
And trouble deaf heaven with my bootless cries,
And look upon myself, and curse my fate,
Wishing me like to one more rich in hope,
Featured like him, like him with friends possessed,
Desiring this man's art and that man's scope,
With what I most enjoy contented least:
Yet in these thoughts myself almost despising,
Haply I think on thee, and then my state,
Like to the lark at break of day arising
From sullen earth, sings hymns at heaven's gate;
    For thy sweet love rememb'red such wealth brings
    That then I scorn to change my state with kings.

---

fortune: fate; destiny
beweep: to weep over
bootless: useless
featured: looking like; having the features of
art: skill
scope: range of action
haply: by chance

THE BIBLE
AS LITERATURE

CREATION AND FALL

from the King James Bible
Genesis 1–3

CHAPTER 1

1 In the beginning God created the heaven and the earth.

2 And the earth was without form, and void; and darkness was upon the face of the deep. And the Spirit of God moved upon the face of the waters.

3 And God said, "Let there be light": and there was light.

4 And God saw the light, that it was good: and God divided the light from the darkness.

5 And God called the light Day, and the darkness he called Night. And the evening and the morning were the first day.

6 And God said, "Let there be a firmament in the midst of the waters, and let it divide the waters from the waters."

7 And God made the firmament, and divided the waters which were under the firmament from the waters which were above the firmament: and it was so.

8 And God called the firmament Heaven. And the evening and the morning were the second day.

9 And God said, "Let the waters under the heaven be gathered together unto one place, and let the dry land appear": and it was so.

---

void: containing nothing; empty; not filled
firmament: the great arch or expanse above, in which the clouds, stars, etc.,
    appear to be placed; the heavens

10 And God called the dry land Earth; and the gathering together of the waters called he Seas: and God saw that it was good.

11 And God said, "Let the earth bring forth grass, the herb yielding seed, and the fruit tree yielding fruit after his kind, whose seed is in itself, upon the earth": and it was so.

12 And the earth brought forth grass, and herb yielding seed after his kind, and the tree yielding fruit, whose seed was in itself, after his kind: and God saw that it was good.

13 And the evening and the morning were the third day.

14 And God said, "Let there be lights in the firmament of the heaven to divide the day from the night; and let them be for signs, and for seasons, and for days, and years:

15 "And let them be for lights in the firmament of the heaven to give light upon the earth": and it was so.

16 And God made two great lights; the greater light to rule the day, and the lesser light to rule the night: he made the stars also.

17 And God set them in the firmament of the heaven to give light upon the earth,

18 And to rule over the day and over the night, and to divide the light from the darkness: and God saw that it was good.

19 And the evening and the morning were the fourth day.

20 And God said, "Let the waters bring forth abundantly the moving creature that hath life, and fowl that may fly above the earth in the open firmament of heaven."

21 And God created great whales, and every living creature that moveth, which the waters brought forth abundantly, after their kind, and every winged fowl after his kind: and God saw that it was good.

22 And God blessed them, saying, "Be fruitful, and multiply, and fill the waters in the seas, and let fowl multiply in the earth."

23 And the evening and the morning were the fifth day.

24 And God said, "Let the earth bring forth the living creature after his kind, cattle, and creeping thing, and beast of the earth after his kind": and it was so.

25 And God made the beast of the earth after his kind, and cattle after their kind, and every thing that creepeth upon the earth after his kind: and God saw that it was good.

26 And God said, "Let us make man in our image, after our likeness: and let them have dominion over the fish of the sea, and over the fowl of the air, and over the cattle, and over all the earth, and over every creeping thing that creepeth upon the earth."

27 So God created man in his own image, in the image of God created he him; male and female created he them.

28 And God blessed them, and God said unto them, "Be fruitful, and multiply, and replenish the earth, and subdue it: and have dominion over the fish of the sea, and over the fowl of the air, and over every living thing that moveth upon the earth."

29 And God said, "Behold, I have given you every herb bearing seed, which is upon the face of all the earth, and every tree, in the which is the fruit of a tree yielding seed; to you it shall be for meat.

---

dominion: control; authority

30 "And to every beast of the earth, and to every fowl of the air, and to every thing that creepeth upon the earth, wherein there is life, I have given every green herb for meat": and it was so.

31 And God saw every thing that he had made, and, behold, it was very good. And the evening and the morning were the sixth day.

CHAPTER 2

1 Thus the heavens and the earth were finished, and all the host of them.

2 And on the seventh day God ended his work which he had made; and he rested on the seventh day from all his work which he had made.

3 And God blessed the seventh day, and sanctified it: because that in it he had rested from all his work which God created and made.

4 These are the generations of the heavens and of the earth when they were created, in the day that the Lord God made the earth and the heavens,

5 And every plant of the field before it was in the earth, and every herb of the field before it grew: for the Lord God had not caused it to rain upon the earth, and there was not a man to till the ground.

6 But there went up a mist from the earth, and watered the whole face of the ground.

7 And the Lord God formed man of the dust of the ground, and breathed into his nostrils the breath of life; and man became a living soul.

8 And the Lord God planted a garden eastward in Eden;
and there he put the man whom he had formed.

9 And out of the ground made the Lord God to grow every
tree that is pleasant to the sight, and good for food; the tree
of life also in the midst of the garden, and the tree of
knowledge of good and evil.

10 And a river went out of Eden to water the garden; and
from thence it was parted, and became into four heads.

11 The name of the first is Pison: that is it which compasseth
the whole land of Havilah, where there is gold;

12 And the gold of that land is good: there is bdellium and
the onyx stone.

13 And the name of the second river is Gihon: the same
is it that compasseth the whole land of Ethiopia.

14 And the name of the third river is Hiddekel: that is
it which goeth toward the east of Assyria. And the fourth
river is Euphrates.

15 And the Lord God took the man, and put him into the
garden of Eden to dress it and to keep it.

16 And the Lord God commanded the man, saying, "Of
every tree of the garden thou mayest freely eat:

17 "But of the tree of the knowledge of good and evil, thou
shalt not eat of it: for in the day that thou eatest thereof thou
shalt surely die."

18 And the Lord God said, "It is not good that the man
should be alone; I will make him an help meet for him."

---

compasseth: surrounds

bdellium: a reddish-brown gum resin similar to myrrh (here, in biblical
    use, may refer to pearls or some precious stone)

onyx: a kind of quartz, used as a gemstone

meet: suitable; fitting ("an help meet for him" means "a helper or
    companion suitable for him," that is, a wife)

19 And out of the ground the Lord God formed every beast of the field, and every fowl of the air; and brought them unto Adam to see what he would call them: and whatsoever Adam called every living creature, that was the name thereof.

20 And Adam gave names to all cattle, and to the fowl of the air, and to every beast of the field; but for Adam there was not found an help meet for him.

21 And the Lord God caused a deep sleep to fall upon Adam, and he slept: and he took one of his ribs, and closed up the flesh instead thereof;

22 And the rib, which the Lord God had taken from man, made he a woman, and brought her unto the man.

23 And Adam said, "This is now bone of my bones, and flesh of my flesh: she shall be called Woman, because she was taken out of Man."

24 Therefore shall a man leave his father and his mother, and shall cleave unto his wife: and they shall be one flesh.

25 And they were both naked, the man and his wife, and were not ashamed.

CHAPTER 3

1 Now the serpent was more subtle than any beast of the field which the Lord God had made. And he said unto the woman, "Yea, hath God said, 'Ye shall not eat of every tree of the garden'?"

2 And the woman said unto the serpent, "We may eat of the fruit of the trees of the garden:

———————

cleave: to hold fast to; to be faithful to; to unite closely in interest or affection
subtle: crafty; cunning

3 "But of the fruit of the tree which is in the midst of the garden, God hath said, 'Ye shall not eat of it, neither shall ye touch it, lest ye die.'"

4 And the serpent said unto the woman, "Ye shall not surely die:

5 "For God doth know that in the day ye eat thereof, then your eyes shall be opened, and ye shall be as gods, knowing good and evil."

6 And when the woman saw that the tree was good for food, and that it was pleasant to the eyes, and a tree to be desired to make one wise, she took of the fruit thereof, and did eat, and gave also unto her husband with her; and he did eat.

7 And the eyes of them both were opened, and they knew that they were naked; and they sewed fig leaves together, and made themselves aprons.

8 And they heard the voice of the Lord God walking in the garden in the cool of the day: and Adam and his wife hid themselves from the presence of the Lord God amongst the trees of the garden.

9 And the Lord God called unto Adam, and said unto him, "Where art thou?"

10 And he said, "I heard thy voice in the garden, and I was afraid, because I was naked; and I hid myself."

11 And he said, "Who told thee that thou wast naked? Hast thou eaten of the tree, whereof I commanded thee that thou shouldest not eat?"

12 And the man said, "The woman whom thou gavest to be with me, she gave me of the tree, and I did eat."

13 And the Lord God said unto the woman, "What is this that thou hast done?" And the woman said, "The serpent beguiled me, and I did eat."

14 And the Lord God said unto the serpent, "Because thou hast done this, thou art cursed above all cattle, and above every beast of the field; upon thy belly shalt thou go, and dust shalt thou eat all the days of thy life:

15 "And I will put enmity between thee and the woman, and between thy seed and her seed; it shall bruise thy head, and thou shalt bruise his heel."

16 Unto the woman he said, "I will greatly multiply thy sorrow and thy conception; in sorrow thou shalt bring forth children; and thy desire shall be to thy husband, and he shall rule over thee."

17 And unto Adam he said, "Because thou hast hearkened unto the voice of thy wife, and hast eaten of the tree, of which I commanded thee, saying, 'Thou shalt not eat of it': cursed is the ground for thy sake; in sorrow shalt thou eat of it all the days of thy life;

18 "Thorns also and thistles shall it bring forth to thee; and thou shalt eat the herb of the field;

19 "In the sweat of thy face shalt thou eat bread, till thou return unto the ground; for out of it wast thou taken: for dust thou art, and unto dust shalt thou return."

20 And Adam called his wife's name Eve; because she was the mother of all living.

21 Unto Adam also and to his wife did the Lord God make coats of skins, and clothed them.

---

beguiled: deceived; tricked
enmity: hostility; hatred
hearkened: listened; paid attention

22 And the Lord God said, "Behold, the man is become as one of us, to know good and evil: and now, lest he put forth his hand, and take also of the tree of life, and eat, and live for ever":
23 Therefore the Lord God sent him forth from the garden of Eden, to till the ground from whence he was taken.
24 So he drove out the man; and he placed at the east of the garden of Eden Cherubims, and a flaming sword which turned every way, to keep the way of the tree of life.

CAIN AND ABEL

from the King James Bible
Genesis 4

1 And Adam knew Eve his wife; and she conceived, and
bare Cain, and said, "I have gotten a man from the Lord."
2 And she again bare his brother Abel. And Abel was a keeper
of sheep, but Cain was a tiller of the ground.

3 And in process of time it came to pass, that Cain brought
of the fruit of the ground an offering unto the Lord.
4 And Abel, he also brought of the firstlings of his flock and
of the fat thereof. And the Lord had respect unto Abel and
to his offering:
5 But unto Cain and to his offering he had not respect. And
Cain was very wroth, and his countenance fell.
6 And the Lord said unto Cain, "Why art thou wroth? and
why is thy countenance fallen?
7 "If thou doest well, shalt thou not be accepted? and if thou
doest not well, sin lieth at the door. And unto thee shall be
his desire, and thou shalt rule over him."
8 And Cain talked with Abel his brother: and it came to pass,
when they were in the field, that Cain rose up against Abel
his brother, and slew him.

---

bare: bore (past tense of *bear*), that is, gave birth to a child
tiller: a person who farms or cultivates land
firstlings: the first offspring
wroth: extremely angry
countenance: appearance; expression; face

9 And the Lord said unto Cain, "Where is Abel thy brother?" And he said, "I know not: Am I my brother's keeper?"

10 And he said, "What hast thou done? the voice of thy brother's blood crieth unto me from the ground.

11 "And now art thou cursed from the earth, which hath opened her mouth to receive thy brother's blood from thy hand;

12 "When thou tillest the ground, it shall not henceforth yield unto thee her strength; a fugitive and a vagabond shalt thou be in the earth."

13 And Cain said unto the Lord, "My punishment is greater than I can bear.

14 "Behold, thou hast driven me out this day from the face of the earth; and from thy face shall I be hid; and I shall be a fugitive and a vagabond in the earth; and it shall come to pass, that every one that findeth me shall slay me."

15 And the Lord said unto him, "Therefore whosoever slayeth Cain, vengeance shall be taken on him sevenfold." And the Lord set a mark upon Cain, lest any finding him should kill him.

16 And Cain went out from the presence of the Lord, and dwelt in the land of Nod, on the east of Eden.

---

fugitive: one who is fleeing or running away from something
vagabond: a wanderer; one who has no permanent home

THREE PSALMS
from the King James Bible

PSALM 8

1 O Lord our Lord, how excellent is thy name in all the earth! who hast set thy glory above the heavens.

2 Out of the mouth of babes and sucklings hast thou ordained strength because of thine enemies, that thou mightest still the enemy and the avenger.

3 When I consider thy heavens, the work of thy fingers, the moon and the stars, which thou hast ordained;

4 What is man, that thou art mindful of him? and the son of man, that thou visitest him?

5 For thou hast made him a little lower than the angels, and hast crowned him with glory and honor.

6 Thou madest him to have dominion over the works of thy hands; thou hast put all things under his feet:

7 All sheep and oxen, yea, and the beasts of the field;

8 The fowl of the air, and the fish of the sea, and whatsoever passeth through the paths of the seas.

9 O Lord our Lord, how excellent is thy name in all the earth!

---

sucklings: babies who are still nursing
ordained: ordered; established
still: to subdue; to make still
avenger: one who seeks revenge
mindful of: attentive to; regardful of; aware of
dominion: control; authority

1 The heavens declare the glory of God; and the firmament sheweth his handywork.

2 Day unto day uttereth speech, and night unto night sheweth knowledge.

3 There is no speech nor language, where their voice is not heard.

4 Their line is gone out through all the earth, and their words to the end of the world. In them hath he set a tabernacle for the sun,

5 Which is as a bridegroom coming out of his chamber, and rejoiceth as a strong man to run a race.

6 His going forth is from the end of the heaven, and his circuit unto the ends of it: and there is nothing hid from the heat thereof.

7 The law of the Lord is perfect, converting the soul: the testimony of the Lord is sure, making wise the simple.

8 The statutes of the Lord are right, rejoicing the heart: the commandment of the Lord is pure, enlightening the eyes.

9 The fear of the Lord is clean, enduring for ever: the judgments of the Lord are true and righteous altogether.

---

firmament: the great arch or expanse above, in which the clouds, stars, etc., appear to be placed; the heavens

sheweth: shows

their line: their call

tabernacle: a place of worship; a portable shrine or sacred tent erected for worship

circuit: a path or route

testimony: a statement; a declaration (in this biblical usage, the sacred scriptures)

statutes: laws

10 More to be desired are they than gold, yea, than much fine gold: sweeter also than honey and the honeycomb.

11 Moreover by them is thy servant warned: and in keeping of them there is great reward.

12 Who can understand his errors? cleanse thou me from secret faults.

13 Keep back thy servant also from presumptuous sins; let them not have dominion over me: then shall I be upright, and I shall be innocent from the great transgression.

14 Let the words of my mouth, and the meditation of my heart, be acceptable in thy sight, O Lord, my strength, and my redeemer.

---

presumptuous: arrogant; foolhardy
transgression: a sin; an offense
meditation: deep thought; serious contemplation

Psalm 23

1 The Lord is my shepherd; I shall not want.

2 He maketh me to lie down in green pastures: he leadeth
me beside the still waters.

3 He restoreth my soul: he leadeth me in the paths
of righteousness for his name's sake.

4 Yea, though I walk through the valley of the shadow of
death, I will fear no evil: for thou art with me; thy rod and
thy staff they comfort me.

5 Thou preparest a table before me in the presence of
mine enemies: thou anointest my head with oil; my cup
runneth over.

6 Surely goodness and mercy shall follow me all the days
of my life: and I will dwell in the house of the Lord for ever.

---

want: to lack; to be in need; to be without

rod and staff: implements used by the shepherd to protect and guide his
　　flock (the terms, which are variously defined in different interpretations
　　of the Bible, may be synonyms for one thing, such as the shepherd's
　　crook, a long stick with a curved end)

anointest: to apply oil to

Faith, Hope, Charity
1 Corinthians 13

King James Version

1 Though I speak with the tongues of men and of angels, and have not charity, I am become as sounding brass, or a tinkling cymbal.

2 And though I have the gift of prophecy, and understand all mysteries, and all knowledge; and though I have all faith, so that I could remove mountains, and have not charity, I am nothing.

3 And though I bestow all my goods to feed the poor, and though I give my body to be burned, and have not charity, it profiteth me nothing.

4 Charity suffereth long, and is kind; charity envieth not; charity vaunteth not itself, is not puffed up,

5 Doth not behave itself unseemly, seeketh not her own, is not easily provoked, thinketh no evil;

6 Rejoiceth not in iniquity, but rejoiceth in the truth;

7 Beareth all things, believeth all things, hopeth all things, endureth all things.

---

charity: unconditional love; universal benevolence; goodwill toward all
prophecy: the ability to predict the future
vaunteth: boasts
unseemly: improperly; rudely
iniquity: wickedness; evil doings

8 Charity never faileth: but whether there be prophecies, they shall fail; whether there be tongues, they shall cease; whether there be knowledge, it shall vanish away.

9 For we know in part, and we prophesy in part.

10 But when that which is perfect is come, then that which is in part shall be done away.

11 When I was a child, I spake as a child, I understood as a child, I thought as a child: but when I became a man, I put away childish things.

12 For now we see through a glass, darkly; but then face to face: now I know in part; but then shall I know even as also I am known.

13 And now abideth faith, hope, charity, these three; but the greatest of these is charity.

Revised Standard Version

1 If I speak in the tongues of men and of angels, but have not love, I am a noisy gong or a clanging cymbal.

2 And if I have prophetic powers, and understand all mysteries and all knowledge, and if I have all faith, so as to remove mountains, but have not love, I am nothing.

3 If I give away all I have, and if I deliver my body to be burned, but have not love, I gain nothing.

4 Love is patient and kind; love is not jealous or boastful;

5 it is not arrogant or rude. Love does not insist on its own way; it is not irritable or resentful;

---

spake: spoke
darkly: with imperfect light, clearness, or knowledge; obscurely; dimly; uncertainly
abideth: endures; lasts

6 it does not rejoice at wrong, but rejoices in the right.

7 Love bears all things, believes all things, hopes all things, endures all things.

8 Love never ends; as for prophecies, they will pass away; as for tongues, they will cease; as for knowledge, it will pass away.

9 For our knowledge is imperfect and our prophecy is imperfect;

10 but when the perfect comes, the imperfect will pass away.

11 When I was a child, I spoke like a child, I thought like a child, I reasoned like a child; when I became a man, I gave up childish ways.

12 For now we see in a mirror dimly, but then face to face. Now I know in part; then I shall understand fully, even as I have been fully understood.

13 So faith, hope, love abide, these three; but the greatest of these is love.

THREE PARABLES
from the Revised Standard Version of the Bible

THE GREAT BANQUET
Luke 14: 16–24

16 But he said to him, "A man once gave a great banquet, and invited many;

17 and at the time for the banquet he sent his servant to say to those who had been invited, 'Come; for all is now ready.'

18 But they all alike began to make excuses. The first said to him, 'I have bought a field, and I must go out and see it; I pray you, have me excused.'

19 And another said, 'I have bought five yoke of oxen, and I go to examine them; I pray you, have me excused.'

20 And another said, 'I have married a wife, and therefore I cannot come.'

21 So the servant came and reported this to his master. Then the householder in anger said to his servant, 'Go out quickly to the streets and lanes of the city, and bring in the poor and maimed and blind and lame.'

22 And the servant said, 'Sir, what you commanded has been done, and still there is room.'

23 And the master said to the servant, 'Go out to the highways and hedges, and compel people to come in, that my house may be filled.

24 For I tell you, none of those men who were invited shall taste my banquet.'"

---

maimed: badly injured; crippled
compel: to drive or urge with force

THE LOST SHEEP AND THE LOST COIN
Luke 15: 1–10

1 Now the tax collectors and sinners were all drawing near
to hear him.

2 And the Pharisees and the scribes murmured, saying,
"This man receives sinners and eats with them."

3 So he told them this parable:

4 "What man of you, having a hundred sheep, if he has lost
one of them, does not leave the ninety-nine in the wilderness,
and go after the one which is lost, until he finds it?

5 And when he has found it, he lays it on his shoulders,
rejoicing.

6 And when he comes home, he calls together his friends
and his neighbors, saying to them, 'Rejoice with me, for I
have found my sheep which was lost.'

7 Just so, I tell you, there will be more joy in heaven over one
sinner who repents than over ninety-nine righteous persons
who need no repentance.

8 Or what woman, having ten silver coins, if she loses one
coin, does not light a lamp and sweep the house and seek
diligently until she finds it?

Pharisees: a group of Jewish leaders in ancient times who were sometimes
  seen as self-righteous because they insisted on very strict observance of
  the scriptural laws
scribes: in ancient times, people whose job it was to write things down
repentance: sorrow and regret for one's misdeeds

9 And when she has found it, she calls together her friends and neighbors, saying, 'Rejoice with me, for I have found the coin which I had lost.'

10 Just so, I tell you, there is joy before the angels of God over one sinner who repents."

THE PRODIGAL SON
Luke 15: 11–32

11 And he said, "There was a man who had two sons;

12 and the younger of them said to his father, 'Father, give me the share of property that falls to me.' And he divided his living between them.

13 Not many days later, the younger son gathered all he had and took his journey into a far country, and there he squandered his property in loose living.

14 And when he had spent everything, a great famine arose in that country, and he began to be in want.

15 So he went and joined himself to one of the citizens of that country, who sent him into his fields to feed swine.

16 And he would gladly have fed on the pods that the swine ate; and no one gave him anything.

17 But when he came to himself he said, 'How many of my father's hired servants have bread enough and to spare, but I perish here with hunger!

18 I will arise and go to my father, and I will say to him, "Father, I have sinned against heaven and before you;

19 I am no longer worthy to be called your son; treat me as one of your hired servants.'

20 And he arose and came to his father. But while he was yet at a distance, his father saw him and had compassion, and ran and embraced him and kissed him.

---

living: the wealth, goods, and property one has earned
squandered: wasted
famine: a shortage of food resulting in widespread hunger and starvation
perish: to die; to waste away

21 And the son said to him, 'Father, I have sinned against heaven and before you; I am no longer worthy to be called your son.'

22 But the father said to his servants, 'Bring quickly the best robe, and put it on him; and put a ring on his hand, and shoes on his feet;

23 and bring the fatted calf and kill it, and let us eat and make merry;

24 for this my son was dead, and is alive again; he was lost, and is found.' And they began to make merry.

25 "Now his elder son was in the field; and as he came and drew near to the house, he heard music and dancing.

26 And he called one of the servants and asked what this meant.

27 And he said to him, 'Your brother has come, and your father has killed the fatted calf, because he has received him safe and sound.'

28 But he was angry and refused to go in. His father came out and entreated him,

29 but he answered his father, 'Lo, these many years I have served you, and I never disobeyed your command; yet you never gave me a kid, that I might make merry with my friends.

30 But when this son of yours came, who has devoured your living with harlots, you killed for him the fatted calf!'

31 And he said to him, 'Son, you are always with me, and all that is mine is yours.

32 It was fitting to make merry and be glad, for this your brother was dead, and is alive; he was lost, and is found.'"

---

entreated: pleaded with

POETRY OF IDEAS

WILL THERE REALLY BE A "MORNING"?

by Emily Dickinson

Will there really be a "Morning"?
Is there such a thing as "Day"?
Could I see it from the mountains
If I were as tall as they?

Has it feet like Water lilies?
Has it feathers like a Bird?
Is it brought from famous countries
Of which I have never heard?

Oh some Scholar! Oh some Sailor!
Oh some Wise Man from the skies!
Please to tell a little Pilgrim
Where the place called "Morning" lies!

---

pilgrim: a traveler to a holy place

I DWELL IN POSSIBILITY

by Emily Dickinson

I dwell in Possibility –
A fairer House than Prose –
More numerous of Windows –
Superior – for Doors –

Of Chambers as the Cedars –
Impregnable of Eye –
And for an Everlasting Roof
The Gambrels of the Sky –

Of Visitors – the fairest –
For Occupation – This –
The spreading wide my narrow Hands
To gather Paradise –

---

prose: ordinary speech or writing, as opposed to poetry
impregnable: difficult to attack or destroy
gambrels: roofs, like barn roofs, that slope on each side, or the angled
    frames that support such roofs

OZYMANDIAS
by Percy Bysshe Shelley

I met a traveler from an antique land,
Who said—"Two vast and trunkless legs of stone
Stand in the desert.... Near them, on the sand,
Half sunk a shattered visage lies, whose frown,
And wrinkled lip, and sneer of cold command,
Tell that its sculptor well those passions read
Which yet survive, stamped on these lifeless things,
The hand that mocked them, and the heart that fed;
And on the pedestal, these words appear:
My name is Ozymandias, King of Kings,
Look on my Works, ye Mighty, and despair!
Nothing beside remains. Round the decay
Of that colossal Wreck, boundless and bare
The lone and level sands stretch far away."

antique: of or from ancient times
visage: face; appearance of a person
colossal: gigantic; enormous

Do Not Go Gentle into That Good Night

by Dylan Thomas

Do not go gentle into that good night,
Old age should burn and rave at close of day;
Rage, rage against the dying of the light.

Though wise men at their end know dark is right,
Because their words had forked no lightning they
Do not go gentle into that good night.

Good men, the last wave by, crying how bright
Their frail deeds might have danced in a green bay,
Rage, rage against the dying of the light.

Wild men who caught and sang the sun in flight,
And learn, too late, they grieved it on its way,
Do not go gentle into that good night.

Grave men, near death, who see with blinding sight
Blind eyes could blaze like meteors and be gay,
Rage, rage against the dying of the light.

And you, my father, there on the sad height,
Curse, bless, me now with your fierce tears, I pray.
Do not go gentle into that good night.
Rage, rage against the dying of the light.

---

rave: to rage; to speak or act wildly

THE CHARGE OF THE LIGHT BRIGADE

by Alfred, Lord Tennyson

1

Half a league, half a league,
Half a league onward,
All in the valley of Death
   Rode the six hundred.
"Forward the Light Brigade!
Charge for the guns!" he said.
Into the valley of Death
   Rode the six hundred.

2

"Forward, the Light Brigade!"
Was there a man dismayed?
Not though the soldier knew
   Someone had blundered.
Theirs not to make reply,
Theirs not to reason why,
Theirs but to do and die.
Into the valley of Death
   Rode the six hundred.

Light Brigade: British cavalry troops who met with disaster during a battle
   in the Crimean War in 1854
league: a distance of about three miles

3

Cannon to right of them,
Cannon to left of them,
Cannon in front of them
   Volleyed and thundered;
Stormed at with shot and shell,
Boldly they rode and well,
Into the jaws of Death,
Into the mouth of hell
   Rode the six hundred.

4

Flashed all their sabers bare,
Flashed as they turned in air
Sab'ring the gunners there,
Charging an army, while
   All the world wondered.
Plunged in the battery smoke
Right through the line they broke;
Cossack and Russian
Reeled from the saber stroke
   Shattered and sundered.
Then they rode back, but not,
   Not the six hundred.

---

volleyed: simultaneously fired
shot: matter fired from a cannon
shell: a bombshell
sabers: swords
battery: a group of army artillery
Cossack: a soldier from a region in southeast Russia
sundered: broken apart; torn apart

5

Cannon to right of them,
Cannon to left of them,
Cannon behind them
   Volleyed and thundered;
Stormed at with shot and shell,
While horse and hero fell,
They that had fought so well
Came through the jaws of Death,
Back from the mouth of hell,
All that was left of them,
   Left of six hundred.

6

When can their glory fade?
O the wild charge they made!
   All the world wondered.
Honor the charge they made!
Honor the Light Brigade,
   Noble six hundred!

THE BATTLE OF BLENHEIM
by Robert Southey

It was a summer evening,
   Old Kaspar's work was done,
And he before his cottage door
   Was sitting in the sun,
And by him sported on the green
His little grandchild Wilhelmine.

She saw her brother Peterkin
   Roll something large and round,
Which he beside the rivulet
   In playing there had found;
He came to ask what he had found,
That was so large, and smooth, and round.

Old Kaspar took it from the boy,
   Who stood expectant by;
And then the old man shook his head,
   And, with a natural sigh,
"'Tis some poor fellow's skull," said he,
"Who fell in the great victory.

Blenheim: now a part of modern Germany, the site of a major battle in
   1704 during the War of Spanish Succession
sported: played
rivulet: a small stream

"I find them in the garden,
    For there's many here about;
And often, when I go to plow,
    The plowshare turns them out!
For many thousand men," said he,
"Were slain in that great victory."

"Now tell us what 'twas all about,"
    Young Peterkin, he cries;
And little Wilhelmine looks up
    With wonder-waiting eyes;
"Now tell us all about the war,
And what they fought each other for."

"It was the English," Kaspar cried,
    "Who put the French to rout;
But what they fought each other for,
    I could not well make out;
But everybody said," quoth he,
"That 'twas a famous victory.

"My father lived at Blenheim then,
    Yon little stream hard by;
They burnt his dwelling to the ground,
    And he was forced to fly;
So with his wife and child he fled,
Nor had he where to rest his head.

---

plowshare: the wedge-shaped steel cutting blade of a plow
put ... to rout: forced into a disorderly retreat
quoth: said
yon: yonder

"With fire and sword the country round
    Was wasted far and wide,
And many a childing mother then,
    And new-born baby died;
But things like that, you know, must be
At every famous victory.

"They say it was a shocking sight
    After the field was won;
For many thousand bodies here
    Lay rotting in the sun;
But things like that, you know, must be
After a famous victory.

"Great praise the Duke of Marlbro' won,
    And our good Prince Eugene."
"Why, 'twas a very wicked thing!"
    Said little Wilhelmine.
"Nay… nay… my little girl," quoth he,
"It was a famous victory.

"And everybody praised the Duke
    Who this great fight did win."
"But what good came of it at last?"
    Quoth little Peterkin.
"Why that I cannot tell," said he;
"But 'twas a famous victory."

Duke of Marlbro': John Churchill, Duke of Marlborough, leading general
    of the combined English and Austrian forces that won the Battle of
    Blenheim in 1704
Prince Eugene: Prince Eugene of Savoy, the Austrian general with whom
    the Duke of Marlborough joined forces

TWO GREAT SPEECHES

THE GETTYSBURG ADDRESS

*An address delivered by President Abraham Lincoln at the
dedication of the Cemetery at Gettysburg, November 19, 1863*

Four score and seven years ago our fathers brought forth
on this continent, a new nation, conceived in Liberty, and
dedicated to the proposition that all men are created equal.

Now we are engaged in a great civil war, testing whether
that nation, or any nation so conceived and so dedicated, can
long endure. We are met on a great battle-field of that war.
We have come to dedicate a portion of that field, as a final
resting place for those who here gave their lives that that
nation might live. It is altogether fitting and proper that
we should do this.

But, in a larger sense, we can not dedicate—we can not
consecrate—we can not hallow—this ground. The brave men,
living and dead, who struggled here, have consecrated it, far
above our poor power to add or detract. The world will little
note, nor long remember what we say here, but it can never
forget what they did here. It is for us the living, rather, to be
dedicated here to the unfinished work which they who fought
here have thus far so nobly advanced. It is rather for us to be

---

four score: 80 (one score is equal to 20)
proposition: a statement of an idea or principle; a proposal
endure: to last; to continue to exist despite hardships
consecrate: to declare as sacred
hallow: to make holy; to set apart as worthy of reverence
detract: to lessen; to take away from

here dedicated to the great task remaining before us—that from these honored dead we take increased devotion to that cause for which they gave the last full measure of devotion—that we here highly resolve that these dead shall not have died in vain—that this nation, under God, shall have a new birth of freedom—and that government of the people, by the people, for the people, shall not perish from the earth.

---

resolve: to form a purpose; to make a firm decision

I HAVE A DREAM

A speech delivered by the Reverend Martin Luther King, Jr.,
on the steps of the Lincoln Memorial in Washington, D.C.,
August 28, 1963

I am happy to join with you today in what will go down in history as the greatest demonstration for freedom in the history of our nation.

Five score years ago, a great American, in whose symbolic shadow we stand today, signed the Emancipation Proclamation. This momentous decree came as a great beacon light of hope to millions of Negro slaves who had been seared in the flames of withering injustice. It came as a joyous daybreak to end the long night of their captivity.

But one hundred years later, the Negro still is not free. One hundred years later, the life of the Negro is still sadly crippled by the manacles of segregation and the chains of discrimination. One hundred years later, the Negro lives on a lonely island of poverty in the midst of a vast ocean of material prosperity. One hundred years later, the Negro is still languished in the corners of American society and finds himself an exile in his own land. And so we've come here today to dramatize a shameful condition.

---

five score: 100 (one score is equal to 20)
Emancipation Proclamation: a document signed during the Civil War in 1862
    by President Abraham Lincoln, freeing the slaves in the Confederacy
decree: an order; a command
seared: burned
withering: devastating
manacles: metal rings and chains used to confine a person's hands
languished: left neglected and in a miserable state

In a sense we've come to our nation's capital to cash a check. When the architects of our republic wrote the magnificent words of the Constitution and the Declaration of Independence, they were signing a promissory note to which every American was to fall heir. This note was a promise that all men—yes, black men as well as white men—would be guaranteed the unalienable rights of life, liberty, and the pursuit of happiness.

It is obvious today that America has defaulted on this promissory note insofar as her citizens of color are concerned. Instead of honoring this sacred obligation, America has given the Negro people a bad check, a check that has come back marked "insufficient funds."

But we refuse to believe that the bank of justice is bankrupt. We refuse to believe that there are insufficient funds in the great vaults of opportunity of this nation. And so we've come to cash this check, a check that will give us upon demand the riches of freedom and security of justice.

We have also come to his hallowed spot to remind America of the fierce urgency of now. This is no time to engage in the luxury of cooling off or to take the tranquilizing drug of gradualism. Now is the time to make real the promises of democracy. Now is the time to rise from the dark and desolate valley of segregation to the sunlit path of racial justice. Now

---

promissory note: a written promise for a future payment;
    a binding agreement
unalienable: incapable of being taken away
defaulted: failed to meet an obligation; failed to make a payment
hallowed: holy; sacred
gradualism: moving toward a goal through a series of small steps; little
    by little
desolate: dismal; dreary; forsaken

is the time to lift our nation from the quicksands of racial injustice to the solid rock of brotherhood. Now is the time to make justice a reality for all of God's children.

It would be fatal for the nation to overlook the urgency of the moment. This sweltering summer of the Negro's legitimate discontent will not pass until there is an invigorating autumn of freedom and equality. Nineteen sixty-three is not an end but a beginning. Those who hoped that the Negro needed to blow off steam and will now be content will have a rude awakening if the nation returns to business as usual. There will be neither rest nor tranquility in America until the Negro is granted his citizenship rights. The whirlwinds of revolt will continue to shake the foundations of our nation until the bright day of justice emerges.

But there is something that I must say to my people who stand on the warm threshold which leads into the palace of justice. In the process of gaining our rightful place we must not be guilty of wrongful deeds. Let us not seek to satisfy our thirst for freedom by drinking from the cup of bitterness and hatred. We must forever conduct our struggle on the high plane of dignity and discipline. We must not allow our creative protest to degenerate into physical violence. Again and again we must rise to the majestic heights of meeting physical force with soul force. The marvelous new militancy which has engulfed the Negro community must not lead us to a distrust of all white people, for many of our white brothers, as evidenced by their presence here today, have come to realize that their destiny is tied up with our destiny. And they have come to realize that

---

invigorating: filling with strength or energy
degenerate: to decline; to sink to a lower state
militancy: an aggressive, fighting spirit or attitude

their freedom is inextricably bound to our freedom. We cannot walk alone.

And as we walk, we must make the pledge that we shall always march ahead. We cannot turn back. There are those who are asking the devotees of civil rights, "When will you be satisfied?" We can never be satisfied as long as the Negro is the victim of the unspeakable horrors of police brutality. We can never be satisfied as long as our bodies, heavy with the fatigue of travel, cannot gain lodging in the motels of the highways and the hotels of the cities. We cannot be satisfied as long as the Negro's basic mobility is from a smaller ghetto to a larger one. We can never be satisfied as long as our children are stripped of their selfhood and robbed of their dignity by signs stating "for whites only." We cannot be satisfied as long as a Negro in Mississippi cannot vote and a Negro in New York believes he has nothing for which to vote. No, no we are not satisfied and we will not be satisfied until justice rolls down like waters and righteousness like a mighty stream.

I am not unmindful that some of you have come here out of great trials and tribulations. Some of you have come fresh from narrow jail cells. Some of you have come from areas where your quest for freedom left you battered by storms of persecution and staggered by the winds of police brutality. You have been the veterans of creative suffering. Continue to work with the faith that unearned suffering is redemptive.

Go back to Mississippi, go back to Alabama, go back to South Carolina, go back to Georgia, go back to Louisiana, go

---

inextricably: inseparably
unmindful: not attentive; unaware
tribulations: suffering; great troubles
redemptive: tending to redeem, that is, to save, rescue, liberate

back to the slums and ghettos of our northern cities, knowing that somehow this situation can and will be changed.

Let us not wallow in the valley of despair. I say to you today my friends—so even though we face the difficulties of today and tomorrow, I still have a dream. It is a dream deeply rooted in the American dream.

I have a dream that one day this nation will rise up and live out the true meaning of its creed: "We hold these truths to be self-evident, that all men are created equal."

I have a dream that one day on the red hills of Georgia the sons of former slaves and the sons of former slave owners will be able to sit down together at the table of brotherhood.

I have a dream that one day even the state of Mississippi, a state sweltering with the heat of injustice, sweltering with the heat of oppression, will be transformed into an oasis of freedom and justice.

I have a dream that my four little children will one day live in a nation where they will not be judged by the color of their skin but by the content of their character.

I have a dream today.

I have a dream that one day down in Alabama, with its vicious racists, with its governor having his lips dripping with the words of interposition and nullification—one day right there in Alabama little black boys and black girls will be able to join hands with little white boys and white girls as sisters and brothers.

I have a dream today.

---

interposition: the act of a state putting itself between the federal
    government and its citizens
nullification: the action of a state attempting to prevent the enforcement of
    a U.S. law within its borders

I have a dream that one day every valley shall be exalted, and every hill and mountain shall be made low, the rough places will be made plain, and the crooked places will be made straight, and the glory of the Lord shall be revealed and all flesh shall see it together.

This is our hope. This is the faith that I go back to the South with. With this faith we will be able to hew out of the mountain of despair a stone of hope. With this faith we will be able to transform the jangling discords of our nation into a beautiful symphony of brotherhood. With this faith we will be able to work together, to pray together, to struggle together, to go to jail together, to stand up for freedom together, knowing that we will be free one day.

This will be the day, this will be the day when all of God's children will be able to sing with new meaning, "My country 'tis of thee, sweet land of liberty, of thee I sing. Land where my fathers died, land of the Pilgrim's pride, from every mountainside, let freedom ring!"

And if America is to be a great nation, this must become true. And so let freedom ring from the prodigious hilltops of New Hampshire. Let freedom ring from the mighty mountains of New York. Let freedom ring from the heightening Alleghenies of Pennsylvania.

Let freedom ring from the snow-capped Rockies of Colorado. Let freedom ring from the curvaceous slopes of California.

But not only that: Let freedom ring from Stone Mountain of Georgia.

---

prodigious: extremely impressive; causing amazement

Alleghenies: a mountain range that runs from northern Pennsylvania to southern Virginia

Stone Mountain: a massive granite mountain with a monument to those Confederate soldiers who died during the Civil War

Let freedom ring from Lookout Mountain of Tennessee.

Let freedom ring from every hill and molehill of Mississippi.

From every mountainside, let freedom ring.

And when this happens, and when we allow freedom [to] ring—when we let it ring from every village and every hamlet, from every state and every city, we will be able to speed up that day when all of God's children—black men and white men, Jews and Gentiles, Protestants and Catholics—will be able to join hands and sing in the words of the old Negro spiritual: "Free at last! Free at last! Thank God Almighty, we are free at last!"

Lookout Mountain: a mountain on the border of Tennessee, Georgia, and
    Alabama that was the site of a famous Civil War battle
hamlet: a small village
Gentiles: non-Jewish people

DRAMA:
AN ANCIENT TRAGEDY

ANTIGONE

A Tragedy by Sophocles
translated by Dudley Fitts and Robert Fitzgerald

Characters

ANTIGONE

HAIMON

ISMENE

TEIRESIAS

EURYDICE

A SENTRY

CREON

A MESSENGER

CHORUS

SCENE: *Before the palace of Creon, King of Thebes. A central double door, and two lateral doors. A platform extends the length of the façade, and from this platform three steps lead down into the "orchestra," or chorus-ground.*

TIME: *Dawn of the day after the repulse of the Argive army from the assault on Thebes.*

Argive: in general, of or relating to the Greeks, and in particular, to those from the Greek city of Argos

PROLOGUE

*[ANTIGONE and ISMENE enter
from the central door of the Palace.]*

ANTIGONE: Ismene, dear sister,
You would think that we had already suffered enough
For the curse on Oedipus:
I cannot imagine any grief
That you and I have not gone through. And now—   5
Have they told you of the new decree of our King Creon?

ISMENE: I have heard nothing: I know
That two sisters lost two brothers, a double death
In a single hour; and I know that the Argive army
Fled in the night; but beyond this, nothing.   10

ANTIGONE: I thought so. And that is why I wanted you
To come out here with me. There is something we must do.

ISMENE: Why do you speak so strangely?

ANTIGONE: Listen, Ismene:
Creon buried our brother Eteocles   15
With military honors, gave him a soldier's funeral,
And it was right that he should; but Polyneices,
Who fought as bravely and died as miserably—
They say that Creon has sworn
No one shall bury him, no one mourn for him,   20
But his body must lie in the fields, a sweet treasure
For carrion birds to find as they search for food.

---

carrion birds: birds, such as vultures, that eat the flesh of dead creatures

That is what they say, and our good Creon is coming here
To announce it publicly; and the penalty—
Stoning to death in the public square! 25
There it is,
And now you can prove what you are:
A true sister, or a traitor to your family.

ISMENE: Antigone, you are mad! What could I possibly do?

ANTIGONE: You must decide whether you will help me or not. 30

ISMENE: I do not understand you. Help you in what?

ANTIGONE: Ismene, I am going to bury him. Will you come?

ISMENE: Bury him! You have just said the new law forbids it.

ANTIGONE: He is my brother. And he is your brother, too.

ISMENE: But think of the danger! Think what Creon will do! 35

ANTIGONE: Creon is not strong enough to stand in my way.

ISMENE: Ah sister!
Oedipus died, everyone hating him
For what his own search brought to light, his eyes
Ripped out by his own hand; and Jocaste died, 40
His mother and wife at once: she twisted the cords
That strangled her life; and our two brothers died,
Each killed by the other's sword. And we are left:
But oh, Antigone,
Think how much more terrible than these 45

Our own death would be if we should go against Creon
And do what he has forbidden! We are only women,
We cannot fight with men, Antigone!
The law is strong, we must give in to the law
In this thing, and in worse. I beg the dead   50
To forgive me, but I am helpless: I must yield
To those in authority. And I think it is dangerous business
To be always meddling.

ANTIGONE: If that is what you think,
I should not want you, even if you asked to come.   55
You have made your choice, you can be what you want to be.
But I will bury him; and if I must die,
I say that this crime is holy: I shall lie down
With him in death, and I shall be as dear
To him as he to me.   60
It is the dead,
Not the living, who make the longest demands:
We die for ever ...
You may do as you like,
Since apparently the laws of the gods mean nothing to you.   65

ISMENE: They mean a great deal to me; but I have no strength
To break laws that were made for the public good.

ANTIGONE: That must be your excuse, I suppose. But
    as for me,
I will bury the brother I love.

ISMENE: Antigone,   70
I am so afraid for you!

ANTIGONE: You need not be:
You have yourself to consider, after all.

ISMENE: But no one must hear of this, you must tell no one!
I will keep it a secret, I promise!   75

ANTIGONE: Oh tell it! Tell everyone!
Think how they'll hate you when it all comes out
If they learn that you knew about it all the time!

ISMENE: So fiery! You should be cold with fear.

ANTIGONE: Perhaps. But I am doing only what I must.   80

ISMENE: But can you do it? I say that you cannot.

ANTIGONE: Very well: when my strength gives out, I shall
    do no more.

ISMENE: Impossible things should not be tried at all.

ANTIGONE: Go away, Ismene: 85
I shall be hating you soon, and the dead will too,
For your words are hateful. Leave me my foolish plan:
I am not afraid of the danger; if it means death,
It will not be the worst of deaths—death without honor.

ISMENE: Go then, if you feel that you must.   90
You are unwise,
But a loyal friend indeed to those who love you.

> [*Exit into the Palace.* ANTIGONE
> *goes off, Left. Enter the* CHORUS.]

PARODOS

CHORUS: [STROPHE 1]
Now the long blade of the sun, lying
Level east to west, touches with glory
Thebes of the Seven Gates. Open, unlidded
Eye of golden day! O marching light
Across the eddy and rush of Dirce's stream,   5
Striking the white shields of the enemy
Thrown headlong backward from the blaze of morning!

CHORAGOS: Polyneices their commander
Roused them with windy phrases,
He the wild eagle screaming   10
Insults above our land,
His wings their shields of snow,
His crest their marshaled helms.

CHORUS: [ANTISTROPHE 1]
Against our seven gates in a yawning ring
The famished spears came onward in the night;   15
But before his jaws were sated with our blood,
Or pinefire took the garland of our towers,

Parodos: the first choral song in the play, which the chorus sings as it enters
strophe: the part of the song sung by the chorus as it moves from right to left
eddy: a current that runs against the main current of a body of water
Dirce: the name of a spring near the city of Thebes
Choragos: the leader of the chorus
marshaled: gathered and put in proper order
helms: helmets used for protection in battle
antistrophe: the part of the song sung by the chorus as it moves from left
    to right
sated: satisfied to excess
pinefire: flaming arrows

He was thrown back; and as he turned, great Thebes—
No tender victim for his noisy power—
Rose like a dragon behind him, shouting war.   20

CHORAGOS: For God hates utterly
The bray of bragging tongues;
And when he beheld their smiling,
Their swagger of golden helms,
The frown of his thunder blasted   25
Their first man from our walls.

CHORUS: [STROPHE 2]
We heard his shout of triumph high in the air
Turn to a scream; far out in a flaming arc
He fell with his windy torch, and the earth struck him.
And others storming in fury no less than his   30
Found shock of death in the dusty joy of battle.

CHORAGOS: Seven captains at seven gates
Yielded their clanging arms to the god
That bends the battle-line and breaks it.
These two only, brothers in blood,   35
Face to face in matchless rage,
Mirroring each the other's death,
Clashed in long combat.

CHORUS: [ANTISTROPHE 2]
But now in the beautiful morning of victory
Let Thebes of the many chariots sing for joy!   40

God: other translations of this play refer instead to "Zeus"; the name is
    used to convey the idea of a supreme deity

With hearts for dancing we'll take leave of war:
Our temples shall be sweet with hymns of praise,
And the long night shall echo with our Chorus:

SCENE I

CHORAGOS: But now at last our new King is coming:
Creon of Thebes, Menoikeus' son.
In this auspicious dawn of his reign
What are the new complexities
That shifting Fate has woven for him?   5
What is his counsel? Why has he summoned
The old men to hear him?

> *[Enter* CREON *from the Palace, Center. He
> addresses the* CHORUS *from the top step.]*

CREON: Gentlemen: I have the honor to inform you that our
Ship of State, which recent storms have threatened to
destroy, has come safely to harbor at last, guided by the   10
merciful wisdom of Heaven. I have summoned you here
this morning because I know that I can depend upon you:
your devotion to King Laios was absolute; you never
hesitated in your duty to our late ruler Oedipus; and
when Oedipus died, your loyalty was transferred to his   15
children. Unfortunately, as you know, his two sons, the
princes Eteocles and Polyneices, have killed each other in
battle; and I, as the next in blood, have succeeded to the
full power of the throne.

---

auspicious: boding well or favorably

I am aware, of course, that no Ruler can expect complete 20
loyalty from his subjects until he has been tested in office.
Nevertheless, I say to you at the very outset that I have
nothing but contempt for the kind of Governor who is
afraid, for whatever reason, to follow the course that he
knows is best for the State; and as for the man who sets 25
private friendship above the public welfare,—I have no use
for him, either. I call God to witness that if I saw my country
headed for ruin, I should not be afraid to speak out plainly;
and I need hardly remind you that I would never have any
dealings with an enemy of the people. No one values 30
friendship more highly than I; but we must remember that
friends made at the risk of wrecking our Ship are not real
friends at all.

These are my principles, at any rate, and that is why I have
made the following decision concerning the sons of 35
Oedipus: Eteocles, who died as a man should die, fighting
for his country, is to be buried with full military honors,
with all the ceremony that is usual when the greatest
heroes die; but his brother Polyneices, who broke his exile
to come back with fire and sword against his native city 40
and the shrines of his fathers' gods, whose one idea was
to spill the blood of his blood and sell his own people into
slavery—Polyneices, I say, is to have no burial: no man is
to touch him or say the least prayer for him; he shall lie on
the plain, unburied; and the birds and the scavenging dogs 45
can do with him whatever they like.

---

exile: banishment

This is my command, and you can see the wisdom behind it. As long as I am King, no traitor is going to be honored with the loyal man. But whoever shows by word and deed that he is on the side of the State,—he shall have my respect 50
while he is living, and my reverence when he is dead.

CHORAGOS: If that is your will, Creon son of Menoikeus,
You have the right to enforce it: we are yours.

CREON: That is my will. Take care that you do your part.

CHORAGOS: We are old men: let the younger ones carry it out. 55

CREON: I do not mean that: the sentries have been appointed.

CHORAGOS: Then what is it that you would have us do?

CREON: You will give no support to whoever breaks this law.

CHORAGOS: Only a crazy man is in love with death!

CREON: And death it is; yet money talks, and the wisest   60
Have sometimes been known to count a few coins too many.
                        [Enter SENTRY from Left.]

SENTRY: I'll not say that I'm out of breath from running, King,
    because every time I stopped to think about what I have to
    tell you, I felt like going back. And all the time a voice kept
    saying, "You fool, don't you know you're walking straight   65

---

reverence: honor; profound respect
sentries: guards

into trouble?"; and then another voice: "Yes, but if you let
somebody else get the news to Creon first, it will be even
worse than that for you!" But good sense won out, at least
I hope it was good sense, and here I am with a story that
makes no sense at all; but I'll tell it anyhow, because, as they   70
say, what's going to happen's going to happen, and—

CREON: Come to the point. What have you to say?

SENTRY: I did not do it. I did not see who did it. You must
    not punish me for what someone else has done.

CREON: A comprehensive defense! More effective, perhaps,   75
    If I knew its purpose. Come: what is it?

SENTRY: A dreadful thing ... I don't know how to put it—

CREON: Out with it!

SENTRY: Well, then;
The dead man—   80
Polyneices—

> *[Pause. The* SENTRY *is overcome, fumbles*
> *for words.* CREON *waits impassively.]*

out there—
someone,—
New dust on the slimy flesh!

> *[Pause. No sign from* CREON.]

Someone has given it burial that way, and   85
Gone ...

---

comprehensive: thorough; including or covering much
impassively: without showing any emotion

[Long pause. CREON *finally speaks with deadly control.]*

CREON: And the man who dared do this?

SENTRY: I swear I
Do not know! You must believe me!
Listen: 90
The ground was dry, not a sign of digging, no,
Not a wheeltrack in the dust, no trace of anyone.
It was when they relieved us this morning: and one of them,
The corporal, pointed to it.
There it was,   95
The strangest—
Look:
The body, just mounded over with light dust: you see?
Not buried really, but as if they'd covered it
Just enough for the ghost's peace. And no sign   100
Of dogs or any wild animal that had been there.
And then what a scene there was! Every man of us
Accusing the other: we all proved the other man did it,
We all had proof that we could not have done it.
We were ready to take hot iron in our hands,   105
Walk through fire, swear by all the gods,
It was not I!
I do not know who it was, but it was not I!

> *[*CREON'S *rage has been mounting steadily,*
> *but the* SENTRY *is too intent upon his*
> *story to notice it.]*

And then, when this came to nothing, someone said
A thing that silenced us and made us stare   110

Down at the ground: you had to be told the news,
And one of us had to do it! We threw the dice,
And the bad luck fell to me. So here I am,
No happier to be here than you are to have me:
Nobody likes the man who brings bad news.   115

CHORAGOS: I have been wondering, King: can it be that the
    gods have done this?

CREON [Furiously]: Stop!
Must you doddering wrecks
Go out of your heads entirely? "The gods!"
Intolerable!   120
The gods favor this corpse? Why? How had he served them?
Tried to loot their temples, burn their images,
Yes, and the whole State, and its laws with it!
Is it your senile opinion that the gods love to honor bad men?
A pious thought!—   125
No, from the very beginning
There have been those who have whispered together,
Stiff-necked anarchists, putting their heads together,
Scheming against me in alleys. These are the men,
And they have bribed my own guard to do this thing.   130

Money! [Sententiously]
There's nothing in the world so demoralizing as money.

---

doddering: shaky and feeble due to age
intolerable: completely unacceptable; unbearable
senile: mentally confused from old age
pious: showing religious devotion
anarchists: people who oppose any government or ruling authority
sententiously: in the manner of a pompous moralizer
demoralizing: corrupting

Down go your cities,
Homes gone, men gone, honest hearts corrupted,
Crookedness of all kinds, and all for money!   135
[To SENTRY*]* But you—!
I swear by God and by the throne of God,
The man who has done this thing shall pay for it!
Find that man, bring him here to me, or your death
Will be the least of your problems: I'll string you up   140
Alive, and there will be certain ways to make you
Discover your employer before you die;
And the process may teach you a lesson you seem
    to have missed:
The dearest profit is sometimes all too dear:
That depends on the source. Do you understand me?   145
A fortune won is often misfortune.

SENTRY: King, may I speak?

CREON: Your very voice distresses me.

SENTRY: Are you sure that it is my voice, and not
    your conscience?

CREON: By God, he wants to analyze me now!   150

SENTRY: It is not what I say, but what has been done,
    that hurts you.

CREON: You talk too much.

---

corrupted: made immoral
discover: to reveal

SENTRY: Maybe; but I've done nothing.

CREON: Sold your soul for some silver: that's all you've done.

SENTRY: How dreadful it is when the right judge judges wrong! 155

CREON: Your figures of speech
May entertain you now; but unless you bring me the man,
You will get little profit from them in the end.
                    [Exit CREON into the Palace.]

SENTRY: "Bring me the man"—!
I'd like nothing better than bringing him the man!   160
But bring him or not, you have seen the last of me here.
At any rate, I am safe!
                    [Exit SENTRY.]

ODE I

CHORUS: *[STROPHE 1]*
Numberless are the world's wonders, but none
More wonderful than man; the storm-gray sea
Yields to his prows, the huge crests bear him high;
Earth, holy and inexhaustible, is graven
With shining furrows where his plows have gone   5
Year after year, the timeless labor of stallions.
                                              [ANTISTROPHE 1]
The lightboned birds and beasts that cling to cover,
The lithe fish lighting their reaches of dim water,

---

furrows: grooves cut in a field by a plow for the planting of seeds
lithe: graceful and slender; moving with ease

All are taken, tamed in the net of his mind;
The lion on the hill, the wild horse windy-maned,   10
Resign to him; and his blunt yoke has broken
The sultry shoulders of the mountain bull.

[STROPHE 2]

Words also, and thought as rapid as air,
He fashions to his good use; statecraft is his,
And his the skill that deflects the arrows of snow,   15
The spears of winter rain: from every wind
He has made himself secure—from all but one:
In the late wind of death he cannot stand.

[ANTISTROPHE 2]

O clear intelligence, force beyond all measure!
O fate of man, working both good and evil!   20
When the laws are kept, how proudly his city stands!
When the laws are broken, what of his city then?
Never may the anarchic man find rest at my hearth,
Never be it said that my thoughts are his thoughts.

SCENE II

[Re-enter SENTRY *leading* ANTIGONE.]

CHORAGOS: What does this mean? Surely this captive woman
Is the Princess, Antigone: Why should she be taken?

SENTRY: Here is the one who did it! We caught her
In the very act of burying him.—Where is Creon?

---

sultry: hot and moist
anarchic: resistant to all authority; opposing any governmental order

CHORAGOS: Just coming from the house. 5
[Enter CREON, Center.]
What has happened?

CREON: Why have you come back so soon?

SENTRY [Expansively]: O King,
A man should never be too sure of anything:
I would have sworn 10
That you'd not see me here again: your anger
Frightened me so, and the things you threatened me with;
But how could I tell then
That I'd be able to solve the case so soon?
No dice throwing this time: I was only too glad to come! 15
Here is this woman. She is the guilty one:
We found her trying to bury him,
Take her, then; question her; judge her as you will.
I am through with the whole thing now, and glad of it.

CREON: But this is Antigone! Why have you brought her here? 20

SENTRY: She was burying him, I tell you!

CREON [Severely]: Is this the truth?

SENTRY: I saw her with my own eyes. Can I say more?

CREON: The details: come, tell me quickly!

SENTRY: It was like this: 25
After those terrible threats of yours, King,
We went back and brushed the dust away from the body.

The flesh was soft by now, and stinking,
So we sat on a hill to windward and kept guard.
No napping this time! We kept each other awake.   30
But nothing happened until the white round sun
Whirled in the center of the round sky over us:
Then, suddenly,
A storm of dust roared up from the earth, and the sky
Went out, the plain vanished with all its trees   35
In the stinging dark. We closed our eyes and endured it.
The whirlwind lasted a long time, but it passed;
And then we looked, and there was Antigone!
I have seen
A mother bird come back to a stripped nest, heard   40
Her crying bitterly a broken note or two
For the young ones stolen. Just so, when this girl
Found the bare corpse, and all her love's work wasted,
She wept, and cried on heaven to damn the hands
That had done this thing.   45
And then she brought more dust
And sprinkled wine three times for her brother's ghost.
We ran and took her at once. She was not afraid,
Not even when we charged her with what she had done.
She denied nothing.   50
And this was a comfort to me,
And some uneasiness: for it is a good thing
To escape from death, but it is no great pleasure
To bring death to a friend.
Yet I always say   55
There is nothing so comfortable as your own safe skin!

---

windward: facing the direction from which the wind is blowing

CREON [*Slowly, dangerously*]: And you, Antigone,
You with your head hanging, do you confess this thing?

ANTIGONE: I do. I deny nothing.

CREON [*To* SENTRY]: You may go.   60
                    [*Exit* SENTRY.]
[*To* ANTIGONE] Tell me, tell me briefly:
Had you heard my proclamation touching this matter?

ANTIGONE: It was public. Could I help hearing it?

CREON: And yet you dared defy the law.

ANTIGONE: I dared.   65
It was not God's proclamation. That final Justice
That rules the world below makes no such laws.
Your edict, King, was strong,
But all your strength is weakness itself against
The immortal unrecorded laws of God.   70
They are not merely now: they were, and shall be,
Operative for ever, beyond man utterly.
I knew I must die, even without your decree:
I am only mortal. And if I must die
Now, before it is my time to die,   75
Surely this is no hardship: can anyone
Living, as I live, with evil all about me,
Think Death less than a friend? This death of mine
Is of no importance; but if I had left my brother
Lying in death unburied, I should have suffered.   80

---

edict: a command

Now I do not.
You smile at me. Ah Creon,
Think me a fool, if you like; but it may well be
That a fool convicts me of folly.

CHORAGOS: Like father, like daughter: both headstrong,   85
    deaf to reason!
She has never learned to yield.

CREON: She has much to learn.
The inflexible heart breaks first, the toughest iron
Cracks first, and the wildest horses bend their necks   90
At the pull of the smallest curb.
Pride? In a slave?
This girl is guilty of a double insolence,
Breaking the given laws and boasting of it.
Who is the man here,   95
She or I, if this crime goes unpunished?
Sister's child, or more than sister's child,
Or closer yet in blood—she and her sister
Win bitter death for this!
[To SERVANTS] Go, some of you,   100
Arrest Ismene: I accuse her equally.
Bring her: you will find her sniffling in the house there.
Her mind's a traitor: crimes kept in the dark
Cry for light, and the guardian brain shudders;
But how much worse than this   105
Is brazen boasting of barefaced anarchy!

ANTIGONE: Creon, what more do you want than my death?

---

insolence: instance of being boldly rude, haughty, or insulting
brazen: scornfully bold; shameless

CREON: Nothing.
That gives me everything.

ANTIGONE: Then I beg you: kill me.
This talking is a great weariness: your words
Are distasteful to me, and I am sure that mine   110
Seem so to you. And yet they should not seem so:
I should have praise and honor for what I have done.
All these men here would praise me
Were their lips not frozen shut with fear of you.
[Bitterly] Ah, the good fortune of kings,   115
Licensed to say and do whatever they please!

CREON: You are alone here in that opinion.

ANTIGONE: No, they are with me. But they keep their
    tongues in leash.

CREON: Maybe. But you are guilty, and they are not.

ANTIGONE: There is no guilt in reverence for the dead.   120

CREON: But Eteocles—was he not your brother too?

ANTIGONE: My brother too.

CREON: And you insult his memory.

ANTIGONE [Softly]: The dead man would not say that I insult it.

CREON: He would: for you honor a traitor as much as him.   125

ANTIGONE: His own brother, traitor or not, and equal in blood.

CREON: He made war on his country. Eteocles defended it.

ANTIGONE: Nevertheless, there are honors due all the dead.

CREON: But not the same for the wicked as for the just.

ANTIGONE: Ah Creon, Creon,   130
Which of us can say what the gods hold wicked?

CREON: An enemy is an enemy, even dead.

ANTIGONE: It is my nature to join in love, not hate.

CREON [*Finally losing patience*]: Go join them, then; if you
    must have your love,
Find it in hell!   135

CHORAGOS: But see, Ismene comes:
                    [*Enter* ISMENE, *guarded.*]
Those tears are sisterly, the cloud
That shadows her eyes rains down gentle sorrow.

CREON: You too, Ismene,
Snake in my ordered house, sucking my blood   140
Stealthily—and all the time I never knew
That these two sisters were aiming at my throne!
Ismene,
Do you confess your share in this crime, or deny it?
Answer me.   145

———————————————

stealthily: sneakily

ISMENE: Yes, if she will let me say so. I am guilty.

ANTIGONE [*Coldly*]: No, Ismene: You have no right to say so.
You would not help me, and I will not have you help me.

ISMENE: But now I know what you meant; and I am here
To join you, to take my share of punishment.   150

ANTIGONE: The dead man and the gods who rule the dead
Know whose act this was. Words are not friends.

ISMENE: Do you refuse me, Antigone? I want to die with you:
I too have a duty that I must discharge to the dead.

ANTIGONE: You shall not lessen my death by sharing it.   155

ISMENE: What do I care for life when you are dead?

ANTIGONE: Ask Creon. You're always hanging on his opinions.

ISMENE: You are laughing at me. Why, Antigone?

ANTIGONE: It's a joyless laughter, Ismene.

ISMENE: But can I do nothing?   160

ANTIGONE: Yes. Save yourself. I shall not envy you.
There are those who will praise you; I shall have honor, too.

ISMENE: But we are equally guilty!

---

discharge: to complete a task one is expected or bound by duty to do

ANTIGONE: No more, Ismene:
You are alive, but I belong to Death.   165

CREON [To the CHORUS]: Gentlemen, I beg you to observe
    these girls:
One has just now lost her mind; the other,
It seems, has never had a mind at all.

ISMENE: Grief teaches the steadiest minds to waver, King.

CREON: Yours certainly did, when you assumed guilt with   170
    the guilty!

ISMENE: But how could I go on living without her?

CREON: You are.
She is already dead.

ISMENE: But your own son's bride!

CREON: There are places enough for him to push his plow.   175
I want no wicked women for my sons!

ISMENE: O dearest Haimon, how your father wrongs you!

CREON: I've had enough of your childish talk of marriage!

CHORAGOS: Do you really intend to steal this girl from
    your son?

---

assumed: took upon oneself

CREON: No; Death will do that for me.   180

CHORAGOS: Then she must die?

CREON [*Ironically*]: You dazzle me.
 —But enough of this talk!
[*To* GUARDS] You, there, take them away and guard them well:
For they are but women, and even brave men run   185
When they see Death coming.
                            [*Exeunt* ISMENE, ANTIGONE,
                            and GUARDS.]

ODE II

CHORUS: [STROPHE 1]
Fortunate is the man who has never tasted God's vengeance!
Where once the anger of heaven has struck, that house is shaken
For ever: damnation rises behind each child
Like a wave cresting out of the black northeast,
When the long darkness under sea roars up   5
And bursts drumming death upon the windwhipped sand.
                                           [ANTISTROPHE 1]
I have seen this gathering sorrow from time long past
Loom upon Oedipus' children: generation from generation
Takes the compulsive rage of the enemy god.
So lately this last flower of Oedipus' line   10
Drank the sunlight! but now a passionate word
And a handful of dust have closed up all its beauty.

---

compulsive: as if driven, compelled, or obsessed

What mortal arrogance,
   Transcends the wrath of Zeus?
Sleep cannot lull him, nor the effortless long months   15
Of the timeless gods: but he is young for ever,
And his house is the shining day of high Olympus.
   All that is and shall be,
   And all the past, is his.

[ANTISTROPHE 2]

No pride on earth is free of the curse of heaven.   20
   The straying dreams of men
   May bring them ghosts of joy:
But as they drowse, the waking embers burn them;
Or they walk with fixed eyes, as blind men walk.
But the ancient wisdom speaks for our own time: 25
   Fate works most for woe
   With Folly's fairest show.
Man's little pleasure is the spring of sorrow.

SCENE III

CHORAGOS: But here is Haimon, King, the last of all your sons.
Is it grief for Antigone that brings him here,
And bitterness at being robbed of his bride?
   [Enter HAIMON.*]*

CREON: We shall soon see, and no need of diviners.—Son,
You have heard my final judgment on that girl: 5

---

arrogance: a feeling of superiority; haughtiness; conceited pride
transcends: goes beyond; surpasses
diviners: soothsayers; persons who predict the future

Have you come here hating me, or have you come
With deference and with love, whatever I do?

HAIMON: I am your son, father. You are my guide.
You make things clear for me, and I obey you.
No marriage means more to me than your continuing wisdom.   10

CREON: Good. That is the way to behave: subordinate
Everything else, my son, to your father's will.
This is what a man prays for, that he may get
Sons attentive and dutiful in his house,
Each one hating his father's enemies,   15
Honoring his father's friends. But if his sons
Fail him, if they turn out unprofitably,
What has he fathered but trouble for himself
And amusement for the malicious?
So you are right   20
Not to lose your head over this woman.
Your pleasure with her would soon grow cold, Haimon.
Let her find her husband in Hell!
Of all the people in this city, only she
Has had contempt for my law and broken it.   25
Do you want me to show myself weak before the people?
Or to break my sworn word? No, and I will not.
The woman dies.
I suppose she'll plead "family ties." Well, let her.
If I permit my own family to rebel,   30
How shall I earn the world's obedience?

---

deference: submission; respect
subordinate: to make subject to; to treat as less important
unprofitably: in a way that brings no gain or benefit
malicious: those who are purposefully mean or spiteful

Show me the man who keeps his house in hand,
He's fit for public authority.
I'll have no dealings
With law-breakers, critics of the government: 35
Whoever is chosen to govern should be obeyed—
Must be obeyed, in all things, great and small,
Just and unjust! O Haimon,
The man who knows how to obey, and that man only,
Knows how to give commands when the time comes.   40
You can depend on him, no matter how fast
The spears come: he's a good soldier, he'll stick it out.

Anarchy, anarchy! Show me a greater evil!
This is why cities tumble and the great houses rain down,
This is what scatters armies!   45
No, no: good lives are made so by discipline.
We keep the laws then, and the lawmakers,
And no woman shall seduce us. If we must lose,
Let's lose to a man, at least! Is a woman stronger than we?

CHORAGOS: Unless time has rusted my wits,   50
What you say, King, is said with point and dignity.

HAIMON [Boyishly earnest]: Father:
Reason is God's crowning gift to man, and you are right
To warn me against losing mine. I cannot say—
I hope that I shall never want to say!—that you   55
Have reasoned badly. Yet there are other men
Who can reason, too; and their opinions might be helpful.
You are not in a position to know everything
That people say or do, or what they feel:
Your temper terrifies them—everyone   60

Will tell you only what you like to hear.
But I, at any rate, can listen; and I have heard them
Muttering and whispering in the dark about this girl.
They say no woman has ever, so unreasonably,
Died so shameful a death for a generous act: 65
"She covered her brother's body. Is this indecent?
She kept him from dogs and vultures. Is this a crime?

Death?—She should have all the honor that we can give her!"
This is the way they talk out there in the City.

You must believe me: 70
Nothing is closer to me than your happiness.
What could be closer? Must not any son
Value his father's fortune as his father does his?
I beg you, do not be unchangeable:
Do not believe that you alone can be right.   75
The man who thinks that,
The man who maintains that only he has the power
To reason correctly, the gift to speak, the soul—
A man like that, when you know him, turns out empty.
It is not reason never to yield to reason!   80

In flood time you can see how some trees bend,
And because they bend, even their twigs are safe,
While stubborn trees are torn up, roots and all.
And the same thing happens in sailing:
Make your sheet fast, never slacken, and over you go,   85
Head over heels and under: and there's your voyage.
Forget you are angry! Let yourself be moved!
I know I am young; but please let me say this:
The ideal condition

Would be, I admit, that men should be right by instinct;   90
But since we are all too likely to go astray,
The reasonable thing is to learn from those who can teach.

CHORAGOS: You will do well to listen to him, King,
If what he says is sensible. And you, Haimon,
Must listen to your father.—Both speak well.   95

CREON: You consider it right for a man of my years
   and experience
To go to school to a boy?

HAIMON: It is not right
If I am wrong. But if I am young, and right,
What does my age matter?   100

CREON: You think it right to stand up for an anarchist?

HAIMON: Not at all. I pay no respect to criminals.

CREON: Then she is not a criminal?

HAIMON: The City would deny it, to a man.

CREON: And the City proposes to teach me how to rule?   105

HAIMON: Ah. Who is it that's talking like a boy now?

CREON: My voice is the one voice giving orders in this City!

HAIMON: It is no City if it takes orders from one voice.

CREON: The State is the King!

HAIMON: Yes, if the State is a desert. 110

CREON [*Pause*]: This boy, it seems, has sold out to a woman.

HAIMON: If you are a woman: my concern is only for you.

CREON: So? Your "concern"! In a public brawl with your father!

HAIMON: How about you, in a public brawl with justice?

CREON: With justice, when all that I do is within my rights? 115

HAIMON: You have no right to trample on God's right.

CREON [*Completely out of control*]: Fool, adolescent fool! Taken
    in by a woman!

HAIMON: You'll never see me taken in by anything vile.

CREON: Every word you say is for her!

HAIMON [*Quietly, darkly*]: And for you. 120
And for me. And for the gods under the earth.

CREON: You'll never marry her while she lives.

HAIMON: Then she must die.—But her death will
    cause another.

CREON: Another?
Have you lost your senses? Is this an open threat?   125

HAIMON: There is no threat in speaking to emptiness.

CREON: I swear you'll regret this superior tone of yours!
You are the empty one!

HAIMON: If you were not my father,
I'd say you were perverse.   130

CREON: You girlstruck fool, don't play at words with me!

HAIMON: I am sorry. You prefer silence.

CREON: Now, by God—!
I swear, by all the gods in heaven above us,
You'll watch it, I swear you shall!   135
[To the SERVANTS*]* Bring her out!
Bring the woman out! Let her die before his eyes!
Here, this instant, with her bridegroom beside her!

HAIMON: Not here, no; she will not die here, King.
And you will never see my face again.   140
Go on raving as long as you've a friend to endure you.
                         [Exit HAIMON.*]*

CHORAGOS: Gone, gone.
Creon, a young man in a rage is dangerous!

---

perverse: stubborn and wrongheaded in the face of evidence

CREON: Let him do, or dream to do, more than a man can.
He shall not save these girls from death.   145

CHORAGOS: These girls?
You have sentenced them both?

CREON: No, you are right.
I will not kill the one whose hands are clean.

CHORAGOS: But Antigone?   150

CREON [*Somberly*]: I will carry her far away
Out there in the wilderness, and lock her
Living in a vault of stone. She shall have food,
As the custom is, to absolve the State of her death.
And there let her pray to the gods of hell: They are her   155
    only gods:
Perhaps they will show her an escape from death,
Or she may learn, though late,
That piety shown the dead is pity in vain.
                                          [*Exit* CREON.]

ODE III

CHORUS: [*STROPHE*]
Love, unconquerable
Waster of rich men, keeper
Of warm lights and all-night vigil

---

absolve: to clear of blame or guilt
piety: dutifulness; devotion

In the soft face of a girl:
Sea-wanderer, forest-visitor!   5
Even the pure Immortals cannot escape you,
And mortal man, in his one day's dusk,
Trembles before your glory.

[ANTISTROPHE]

Surely you swerve upon ruin
The just man's consenting heart,   10
As here you have made bright anger
Strike between father and son—
And none has conquered but Love!
A girl's glance working the will of heaven;
Pleasure to her alone who mocks us,   15
Merciless Aphrodite.

SCENE IV

CHORAGOS [As ANTIGONE enters guarded]: But I can no
    longer stand in awe of this,
Nor, seeing what I see, keep back my tears.
Here is Antigone, passing to that chamber
Where all find sleep at last.

[STROPHE 1]

ANTIGONE: Look upon me, friends, and pity me   5
Turning back at the night's edge to say
Good-by to the sun that shines for me no longer;
Now sleepy Death

---

consenting: agreeing
Aphrodite: the Greek goddess of love

Summons me down to Acheron, that cold shore:
There is no bridesong there, nor any music.   10

CHORUS: Yet not unpraised, not without a kind of honor,
You walk at last into the underworld;
Untouched by sickness, broken by no sword.
What woman has ever found your way to death?

[ANTISTROPHE 1]

ANTIGONE: How often I have heard the story of Niobe,   15
Tantalos' wretched daughter, how the stone
Clung fast about her, ivy-close: and they say
The rain falls endlessly
And sifting soft snow; her tears are never done.
I feel the loneliness of her death in mine.   20

CHORUS: But she was born of heaven, and you
Are woman, woman-born. If her death is yours,
A mortal woman's, is this not for you
Glory in our world and in the world beyond?

[STROPHE 2]

ANTIGONE: You laugh at me. Ah, friends, friends,   25
Can you not wait until I am dead? O Thebes,
O men many-charioted, in love with Fortune,
Dear springs of Dirce, sacred Theban grove,

Acheron: the river that the ancient Greeks believed the dead crossed to
   enter Hades, the underworld realm of the dead
Niobe: in Greek mythology, an ancestor of Antigone, a Greek queen and
   mother whose children died and who herself was turned to stone as a
   result of her pride
Tantalos (also spelled *Tantalus*): in Greek mythology, a king who, for
   offending the gods, was punished by being placed in water that drew
   away when he tried to drink, and near fruit that moved out of his reach
   when he tried to eat

Be witnesses for me, denied all pity,
Unjustly judged! and think a word of love   30
For her whose path turns
Under dark earth, where there are no more tears.

CHORUS: You have passed beyond human daring and come
    at last
Into a place of stone where Justice sits.
I cannot tell   35
What shape of your father's guilt appears in this.

                            [ANTISTROPHE 2]

ANTIGONE: You have touched it at last: that bridal bed
Unspeakable, horror of son and mother mingling:
Their crime, infection of all our family!
O Oedipus, father and brother!   40
Your marriage strikes from the grave to murder mine.
I have been a stranger here in my own land:
All my life
The blasphemy of my birth has followed me.

CHORUS: Reverence is a virtue, but strength   45
Lives in established law: that must prevail.
You have made your choice,
Your death is the doing of your conscious hand.

                                   [EPODE]

ANTIGONE: Then let me go, since all your words are bitter,
And the very light of the sun is cold to me.   50
Lead me to my vigil, where I must have
Neither love nor lamentation; no song, but silence.

---

blasphemy: irreverence and disrespect for the gods
epode: literally *"after-song,"* the part of the chorus's song that fo lows
    strophe and antistrophe

[CREON *interrupts impatiently.*]

CREON: If dirges and planned lamentations could put off death,
Men would be singing for ever.
[*To the* SERVANTS] Take her, go!   55
You know your orders: take her to the vault
And leave her alone there. And if she lives or dies,
That's her affair, not ours: our hands are clean.

ANTIGONE: O tomb, vaulted bride-bed in eternal rock,
Soon I shall be with my own again   60
Where Persephone welcomes the thin ghosts underground:
And I shall see my father again, and you, mother,
And dearest Polyneices—dearest indeed
To me, since it was my hand
That washed him clean and poured the ritual wine: 65
And my reward is death before my time!
And yet, as men's hearts know, I have done no wrong,
I have not sinned before God. Or if I have,
I shall know the truth in death. But if the guilt
Lies upon Creon who judged me, then, I pray,   70
May his punishment equal my own.

CHORAGOS: O passionate heart,
Unyielding, tormented still by the same winds!

CREON: Her guards shall have good cause to regret
    their delaying.

---

lamentation: expression of sorrow and grief
dirges: music or songs of mourning performed at a funeral
Persephone: the Greek goddess of the underworld

ANTIGONE: Ah! That voice is like the voice of death!   75

CREON: I can give you no reason to think you are mistaken.

ANTIGONE: Thebes, and you my fathers' gods,
And rulers of Thebes, you see me now, the last
Unhappy daughter of a line of kings,
Your kings, led away to death. You will remember   80
What things I suffer, and at what men's hands,
Because I would not transgress the laws of heaven.
[To the GUARDS, *simply]* Come: let us wait no longer.
                            [Exit ANTIGONE, *Left, guarded.]*

ODE IV

[STROPHE 1]

CHORUS: All Danae's beauty was locked away
In a brazen cell where the sunlight could not come:
A small room, still as any grave, enclosed her.
Yet she was a princess too,
And Zeus in a rain of gold poured love upon her.   5
O child, child,
No power in wealth or war
Or tough sea-blackened ships
Can prevail against untiring Destiny!

---

transgress: to go beyond the bounds of
Danae: in Greek mythology, Danae's father, the king, imprisoned her
    because of a prophecy that she would have a son (Perseus) who would
    cause the death of the king
brazen: made of bronze

And Dryas' son also, that furious king,   10
Bore the god's prisoning anger for his pride:
Sealed up by Dionysos in deaf stone,
His madness died among echoes.
So at the last he learned what dreadful power
His tongue had mocked: 15
For he had profaned the revels,
And fired the wrath of the nine
Implacable Sisters that love the sound of the flute.

And old men tell a half-remembered tale
Of horror done where a dark ledge splits the sea   20
And a double surf beats on the gray shores:
How a king's new woman, sick
With hatred for the queen he had imprisoned,
Ripped out his two sons' eyes with her bloody hands
While grinning Ares watched the shuttle plunge   25
Four times: four blind wounds crying for revenge,

Crying, tears and blood mingled.—Piteously born,
Those sons whose mother was of heavenly birth!
Her father was the god of the North Wind
And she was cradled by gales,   30
She raced with young colts on the glittering hills
And walked untrammeled in the open light:

Dryas: a mad Greek king who punished his son
Dionysos (also spelled *Dionysus*): the Greek god of wine
profaned: treated something sacred with great disrespect
implacable: impossible to soothe or make peace with
Sisters: the nine Muses, the Greek goddesses of the arts and sciences
Ares: the Greek god of war
untrammeled: unrestrained; freely

But in her marriage deathless Fate found means
To build a tomb like yours for all her joy.

SCENE V

[Enter blind TEIRESIAS, *led by a boy. The opening speeches of* TEIRESIAS *should be in singsong contrast to the realistic lines of* CREON.*]*

TEIRESIAS: This is the way the blind man comes,
   Princes, Princes,
Lock-step, two heads lit by the eyes of one.

CREON: What new thing have you to tell us, old Teiresias?

TEIRESIAS: I have much to tell you: listen to the prophet, Creon.

CREON: I am not aware that I have ever failed to listen.   5

TEIRESIAS: Then you have done wisely, King, and ruled well.

CREON: I admit my debt to you. But what have you to say?

TEIRESIAS: This, Creon: you stand once more on the edge
   of fate.

CREON: What do you mean? Your words are a kind of dread.

Teiresias (also spelled *Tiresias*): in Greek mythology, a blind prophet

Teiresias: Listen, Creon: 10
I was sitting in my chair of augury, at the place
Where the birds gather about me. They were all a-chatter,
As is their habit, when suddenly I heard
A strange note in their jangling, a scream, a
Whirring fury; I knew that they were fighting, 15
Tearing each other, dying
In a whirlwind of wings clashing. And I was afraid.
I began the rites of burnt offering at the altar,
But Hephaestos failed me: instead of bright flame,
There was only the sputtering slime of the fat thigh flesh 20
Melting: the entrails dissolved in gray smoke,
The bare bone burst from the welter. And no blaze!

This was a sign from heaven. My boy described it,
Seeing for me as I see for others.

I tell you, Creon, you yourself have brought 25
This new calamity upon us. Our hearths and altars
Are stained with the corruption of dogs and carrion birds
That glut themselves on the corpse of Oedipus' son.
The gods are deaf when we pray to them, their fire
Recoils from our offering, their birds of omen 30
Have no cry of comfort, for they are gorged
With the thick blood of the dead.
O my son,
These are no trifles! Think: all men make mistakes,
But a good man yields when he knows his course is wrong, 35

---

augury: the practice of foretelling events by observing the actions of birds
Hephaestos (also spelled *Hephaestus*): the Greek god of fire and the forge
welter: a confused mass; jumbled matter
calamity: disaster; catastrophe

And repairs the evil. The only crime is pride.

Give in to the dead man, then: do not fight with a corpse—
What glory is it to kill a man who is dead?
Think, I beg you:
It is for your own good that I speak as I do.   40
You should be able to yield for your own good.

CREON: It seems that prophets have made me their
    especial province.
All my life long
I have been a kind of butt for the dull arrows
Of doddering fortune tellers!   45
No, Teiresias:
If your birds—if the great eagles of God himself
Should carry him stinking bit by bit to heaven,
I would not yield. I am not afraid of pollution:
No man can defile the gods.   50
Do what you will,
Go into business, make money, speculate
In India gold or that synthetic gold from Sardis,
Get rich otherwise than by my consent to bury him.
Teiresias, it is a sorry thing when a wise man   55
Sells his wisdom, lets out his words for hire!

TEIRESIAS: Ah Creon! Is there no man left in the world—

CREON: To do what?—Come, let's have the aphorism!

---

their especial province: their particular concern; their chief business
butt: a target (in archery)
defile: to make impure
aphorism: a proverb; a brief wise saying

TEIRESIAS: No man who knows that wisdom outweighs
   any wealth?

CREON: As surely as bribes are baser than any baseness.   60

TEIRESIAS: You are sick, Creon! You are deathly sick!

CREON: As you say: it is not my place to challenge a prophet.

TEIRESIAS: Yet you have said my prophecy is for sale.

CREON: The generation of prophets has always loved gold.

TEIRESIAS: The generation of kings has always loved brass.   65

CREON: You forget yourself! You are speaking to your King.

TEIRESIAS: I know it. You are a king because of me.

CREON: You have a certain skill; but you have sold out.

TEIRESIAS: King, you will drive *me* to words that—

CREON: Say them, say them!   70
Only remember: I will not pay you for them.

TEIRESIAS: No, you will find them too costly.

CREON: No doubt. Speak:
Whatever you say, you will not change my will.

TEIRESIAS: Then take this, and take it to heart! 75
The time is not far off when you shall pay back
Corpse for corpse, flesh of your own flesh.
You have thrust the child of this world into living night,
You have kept from the gods below the child that is theirs:
The one in a grave before her death, the other, 80
Dead, denied the grave. This is your crime:
And the Furies and the dark gods of Hell
Are swift with terrible punishment for you.

Do you want to buy me now, Creon? Not many days,
And your house will be full of men and women weeping, 85
And curses will be hurled at you from far
Cities grieving for sons unburied, left to rot
Before the walls of Thebes.

These are my arrows, Creon: they are all for you.
But come, child: lead me home. *[To* BOY*]* 90

Let him waste his fine anger upon younger men.
Maybe he will learn at last
To control a wiser tongue in a better head.
[Exit TEIRESIAS.*]*

CHORAGOS: The old man has gone, King, but his words
Remain to plague us. I am old, too, 95
But I cannot remember that he was ever false.

Furies: a later Roman name for the Greek goddesses called the Erinyes,
   three winged goddesses of vengeance who horribly punished
   certain crimes

CREON: That is true.... It troubles me.
Oh it is hard to give in! but it is worse
To risk everything for stubborn pride.

CHORAGOS: Creon: take my advice.   100

CREON: What shall I do?

CHORAGOS: Go quickly: free Antigone from her vault
And build a tomb for the body of Polyneices.

CREON: You would have me do this?

CHORAGOS: Creon, yes!   105
And it must be done at once: God moves
Swiftly to cancel the folly of stubborn men.

CREON: It is hard to deny the heart! But I
Will do it: I will not fight with destiny.

CHORAGOS: You must go yourself, you cannot leave it   110
  to others.

CREON: I will go.
—Bring axes, servants:
Come with me to the tomb. I buried her, I
Will set her free.
Oh quickly!   115
My mind misgives—

---

misgives: feels doubt or apprehension

The laws of the gods are mighty, and a man must serve them
To the last day of his life!

[Exit CREON.*]*

PAEAN

[STROPHE 1]

CHORAGOS: God of many names

CHORUS: O Iacchos
son of Kadmeian Semele
O born of the Thunder!
Guardian of the West   5
Regent of Eleusis' plain
O Prince of maenad Thebes
and the Dragon Field by rippling Ismenos:

[ANTISTROPHE 1]

CHORAGOS: God of many names

CHORUS: The flame of torches   10
flares on our hills

---

pacan: a joyous song of praise; in ancient Greece, a hymn of thanksgiving
    to a god
Iacchos: another name for Dionysus
Kadmeian Semele: Dionysus' mother, daughter of Kadmus
Eleusis: a Greek city sacred to the goddesses Persephone and Demeter
maenad: here used as an adjective to mean "raging, frenzied"; from
    Maenads, the priestesses of Dionysos, whose rituals were sometimes
    wild and ecstatic
Ismenos: a river in Thebes

the nymphs of Iacchos
dance at the spring of Castalia:

from the vine-close mountain
come ah come in ivy: 15
Evohé evohé! sings through the streets of Thebes

                                                    [*STROPHE 2*]

CHORAGOS: God of many names

CHORUS: Iacchos of Thebes
heavenly Child
of Semele bride of the Thunderer!   20
The shadow of plague is upon us:
come with clement feet
oh come from Parnassos
down the long slopes
across the lamenting water.   25

                                                    [*ANTISTROPHE 2*]

CHORAGOS: Iô Fire! Chorister of the throbbing stars!
O purest among the voices of the night!
Thou son of God, blaze for us!

---

nymphs: female nature spirits
Castalia: in Greek mythology, a sacred spring
Evohé evohé: a cry of Dionysus' worshippers
clement: merciful; mild
Parnassos (also spelled *Parnassus*): a mountain in Greece, in ancient times
    sacred to Dionysus
Iô: a shout of joy, victory, and celebration
chorister: the leader of a choir

CHORUS: Come with choric rapture of circling Maenads
Who cry *Iô Iacche!*   30
God of many names!

ÉXODOS

[Enter MESSENGER, *Left.]*

MESSENGER: Men of the line of Kadmos, you who live
Near Amphion's citadel:
I cannot say
Of any condition of human life "This is fixed,
This is clearly good, or bad." Fate raises up,   5
And Fate casts down the happy and unhappy alike:
No man can foretell his Fate.
Take the case of Creon:
Creon was happy once, as I count happiness:
Victorious in battle, sole governor of the land,   10
Fortunate father of children nobly born.
And now it has all gone from him! Who can say
That a man is still alive when his life's joy fails?
He is a walking dead man. Grant him rich,
Let him live like a king in his great house: 15
If his pleasure is gone, I would not give
So much as the shadow of smoke for all he owns.

CHORAGOS: Your words hint at sorrow: what is your
    news for us?

Iacche: a form of the name *Iacchos*
Éxodos: the final scene
Amphion's citadel: a fortress in Thebes, believed to have been built by
    Amphion, husband of Niobe

MESSENGER: They are dead. The living are guilty
    of their death.

CHORAGOS: Who is guilty? Who is dead? Speak!   20

MESSENGER: Haimon.
Haimon is dead; and the hand that killed him
Is his own hand.

CHORAGOS: His father's? or his own?

MESSENGER: His own, driven mad by the murder his father   25
    had done.

CHORAGOS: Teiresias, Teiresias, how clearly you saw it all!

MESSENGER: This is my news: you must draw what
    conclusions you can from it.

CHORAGOS: But look: Eurydice, our Queen:
Has she overheard us?
                    [Enter EURYDICE from the Palace, Center.]

EURYDICE: I have heard something, friends: 30
As I was unlocking the gate of Pallas' shrine,
For I needed her help today, I heard a voice
Telling of some new sorrow. And I fainted
There at the temple with all my maidens about me.

_____

Eurydice: the wife of Creon
Pallas: a name for Athena, the Greek goddess of wisdom

But speak again: whatever it is, I can bear it: 35
Grief and I are no strangers.

MESSENGER: Dearest Lady,
I will tell you plainly all that I have seen.
I shall not try to comfort you: what is the use,
Since comfort could lie only in what is not true?   40
The truth is always best.
I went with Creon
To the outer plain where Polyneices was lying,
No friend to pity him, his body shredded by dogs.
We made our prayers in that place to Hecate   45
And Pluto, that they would be merciful. And we bathed
The corpse with holy water, and we brought
Fresh-broken branches to burn what was left of it,
And upon the urn we heaped up a towering barrow
Of the earth of his own land.   50
When we were done, we ran
To the vault where Antigone lay on her couch of stone.
One of the servants had gone ahead,
And while he was yet far off he heard a voice
Grieving within the chamber, and he came back   55
And told Creon. And as the King went closer,
The air was full of wailing, the words lost,
And he begged us to make all haste. "Am I a prophet?"
He said, weeping, "And must I walk this road,
The saddest of all that I have gone before?   60
My son's voice calls me on. Oh quickly, quickly!

Hecate: a Greek goddess associated with the underworld
Pluto: the later Roman name for Hades, the Greek god of the underworld
barrow: a large mound of earth over a burial site

Look through the crevice there, and tell me
If it is Haimon, or some deception of the gods!"

We obeyed; and in the cavern's farthest corner
We saw her lying: 65
She had made a noose of her fine linen veil
And hanged herself. Haimon lay beside her,
His arms about her waist, lamenting her,
His love lost under ground, crying out
That his father had stolen her away from him.   70

When Creon saw him the tears rushed to his eyes
And he called to him: "What have you done, child? Speak
    to me,
What are you thinking that makes your eyes so strange?
O my son, my son, I come to you on my knees!"
But Haimon spat in his face. He said not a word,   75
Staring—
And suddenly drew his sword
And lunged. Creon shrank back, the blade missed; and the boy,
Desperate against himself, drove it half its length
Into his own side, and fell. And as he died   80
He gathered Antigone close in his arms again,
Choking, his blood bright red on her white cheek.
And now he lies dead with the dead, and she is his
At last, his bride in the houses of the dead.

                    [Exit EURYDICE into the Palace.]

CHORAGOS: She has left us without a word. What can   85
    this mean?

MESSENGER: It troubles me, too; yet she knows what is best,
Her grief is too great for public lamentation,
And doubtless she has gone to her chamber to weep
For her dead son, leading her maidens in his dirge.

CHORAGOS: It may be so: but I fear this deep silence.   90

MESSENGER [Pause]: I will see what she is doing. I will go in.
                    [Exit MESSENGER into the Palace.]

                    [Enter CREON with attendants, bearing
                    HAIMON'S body.]

CHORAGOS: But here is the King himself: oh look at him,
Bearing his own damnation in his arms.

CREON: Nothing you say can touch me any more.
My own blind heart has brought me   95
From darkness to final darkness. Here you see
The father murdering, the murdered son—
And all my civic wisdom!

Haimon my son, so young, so young to die,
I was the fool, not you; and you died for me.   100

CHORAGOS: That is the truth; but you were late in learning it.

CREON: This truth is hard to bear. Surely a god
Has crushed me beneath the hugest weight of heaven.
And driven me headlong a barbaric way
To trample out the thing I held most dear.   105
The pains that men will take to come to pain!

[Enter MESSENGER *from the Palace.]*

MESSENGER: The burden you carry in your hands is heavy,
But it is not all: you will find more in your house.

CREON: What burden worse than this shall I find there?

MESSENGER: The Queen is dead. 110

CREON: O port of death, deaf world,
Is there no pity for me? And you, Angel of evil,
I was dead, and your words are death again.
Is it true, boy? Can it be true?
Is my wife dead? Has death bred death? 115

MESSENGER: You can see for yourself.
                    [The doors are opened, and the body of
                    EURYDICE *is disclosed within.]*

CREON: Oh pity!
All true, all true, and more than I can bear!
O my wife, my son!

MESSENGER: She stood before the altar, and her heart 120
Welcomed the knife her own hand guided,
And a great cry burst from her lips for Megareus dead,
And for Haimon dead, her sons; and her last breath
Was a curse for their father, the murderer of her sons.
And she fell, and the dark flowed in through her closing eyes. 125

CREON: O God, I am sick with fear.
Are there no swords here? Has no one a blow for me?

MESSENGER: Her curse is upon you for the deaths of both.

CREON: It is right that it should be. I alone am guilty.
I know it, and I say it. Lead me in,   130
Quickly, friends.
I have neither life nor substance. Lead me in.

CHORAGOS: You are right, if there can be right in
    so much wrong.
The briefest way is best in a world of sorrow.

CREON: Let it come,   135
Let death come quickly, and be kind to me.
I would not ever see the sun again.

CHORAGOS: All that will come when it will; but we,
    meanwhile,
Have much to do. Leave the future to itself.

CREON: All my heart was in that prayer!   140

CHORAGOS: Then do not pray any more: the sky is deaf.

CREON: Lead me away. I have been rash and foolish.
I have killed my son and my wife.
I look for comfort; my comfort lies here dead.
Whatever my hands have touched has come to nothing.   145
Fate has brought all my pride to a thought of dust.

            [As CREON is being led into the house, the
            CHORAGOS advances and speaks directly
            to the audience.]

CHORAGOS: There is no happiness where there is no wisdom;
No wisdom but in submission to the gods.
Big words are always punished,
And proud men in old age learn to be wise.

INDEX OF AUTHORS AND TITLES

ACKNOWLEDGMENTS

THE ANTIGONE OF SOPHOCLES, AN ENGLISH VERSION by Dudley Fitts and Robert Fitzgerald, copyright © 1939 by Harcourt Inc., and renewed 1967 by Dudley Fitts and Robert Fitzgerald, reprinted by permission of the publisher.

From BARRIO BOY by Ernesto Galarza. Copyright © 1971 by University of Notre Dame Press, Notre Dame, Indiana 46556. Used by permission of the publisher.

"Do Not Go Gentle into That Good Night" by Dylan Thomas, from THE POEMS OF DYLAN THOMAS, copyright © 1952 by Dylan Thomas. Reprinted by permission of New Directions Publishing Corp. and David Higham Associates Limited.

"THE GLASS OF MILK" by Manuel Rojas. Reprinted by permission of Rosalie Torres-Rioseco.

"Gumption" from SHORT STORIES by Langston Hughes. Copyright © 1996 by Ramona Bass and Arnold Rampersad. Reprinted by permission of Hill and Wang, a division of Farrar Strauss and Giroux, LLC.

Excerpt from I KNOW WHY THE CAGED BIRD SINGS by Maya Angelou, copyright © 1969 and renewed by Maya Angelou. Used by permission of Random House, Inc.

"in Just" Copyright 1923, 1951, © 1991 by the Trustees for the E. E. Cummings Trust. Copyright © 1976 by George James Firmage, from COMPLETE POEMS: 1904–1962 by E. E. Cummings, edited by George J. Firmage. Used by permission of Liveright Publishing Corporation.

"The Lottery" from THE LOTTERY AND OTHER STORIES by Shirley Jackson. Copyright © 1948, 1949 by Shirley Jackson. Copyright renewed 1976, 1977 by Laurence Hyman, Barry Hyman, Mrs. Sarah Webster and Mrs. Joanne Schnurer. Reprinted by permission of Farrar, Strauss and Giroux, LLC.